JIM KURTZ TAKES US ON AN INCREDIBLE PERSONAL JOURNEY that spans over six decades. He sets out to find the father he never knew and accomplishes that and so much more. We follow the author as he begins to collect the pieces of the puzzle that made up the man who was Robert R. Kurtz. *The Green Box* is set in the past and the present, telling the story of perseverance in the face of overwhelming odds, two men's devotion to family, and the ultimate discovery of what defines the unique relationship that is father and son. As a career, I motivate people. This story motivated me!

—Steven B. Wiley
Founder and President
Lincoln Leadership Institute
Gettysburg, Pennsylvania

THIS BOOK IS AN AMAZING STORY WRITTEN BY A MAN WHO never knew his father except for what he learned from the contents in a green box he found in the attic of his home. His father was a WWII Army Air Force B-24 pilot who was shot down and captured by the Germans. He was moved through various German POW camps and suffered the indignities, filth, hunger, loneliness, and sickness that defined them. Sometimes, war prisoners think that it would be better to die than continue to suffer, especially when there seems to be no end to the suffering. When we wonder, "What is war like?" we should not forget about the POWs. Their bravery is just as significant as all other fighters.

—Brigadier General James L. Anderson, Ret., PhD.

MY DAD WAS NAVIGATOR ON THE SAME B-24 AS THE author's father in WWII. On occasion, he would tell us stories of his war experiences, but I always knew there were many more that were clearly too painful for him to share with me. Jim's book has filled in many of the missing pieces. *The Green Box* also unveils a wonderful wartime romance. The first person remembrances made by the author's mom are most powerful. She is the one who made Jim's dad come alive for me. I listened when she was quoted. Perhaps the greatest part of the love story is that she never remarried.

—Jane Donovan
Daughter of Joseph Spontak

THE
GREEN BOX

2-26-19

To Michael Kosmos,

THE
GREEN BOX

Jim Kurtz

With warmest regards!

Jim Kurtz

KK

IPSWICH, MASSACHUSETTS

PUBLISHED BY KHK
IPSWICH, MASSACHUSETTS

THE GREEN BOX BY JIM KURTZ

ISBN Number: 978-0-692-34942-7
Library of Congress Control Number: 2015930243

COVER AND INTERIOR DESIGN BY JULIE KURTZ AND JEANNE KOLES
PRINTED BY GROSSMAN MARKETING, SOMERVILLE, MA

TO MY SONS, MIKE AND BRIAN, WHO HAVE brought more love and joy into my life than I would ever have thought possible. You have always wanted to know about your grandfather and what type of man he was. I am honored and blessed to now provide you with that opportunity. I love you guys.

CONTENTS

2nd Lieutenant Robert R. Kurtz
Pantanella, Italy, Summer 1944

AUTHOR'S NOTE

T HE GREEN BOX IS THE CULMINATION OF THE SEARCH FOR the details of my father's life. The search itself became a story that demanded to be told. The book blends literary forms: it is part memoir, part biography, and part informed speculation as to my father's experiences and emotions. He spoke little about his trials, and only hinted at them in letters and essays. *The Green Box* moves between past and present, as I weave together interviews with people who knew my father, and accounts of soldiers who endured the same challenges that he did, along with my own imagined scenarios.

As the events of World War II fade more rapidly into the shadows of history with the passing of the last survivors who could tell what happened to them, and what they learned, it is essential that we remember that it was a war, like all wars, fought and experienced by flesh-and-blood people living in desperate times. There were dark moments and moments of hope, atrocities and acts of courage. There were heroes at home who waited and kept the beautifully mundane aspects of life going, people like my mother. And there were the heroes who fought the war, some of whom did not make it back, and some who did, like my father. Their stories make us who we are today. It is my privilege to share what I have learned about my father, and as a result about myself.

I'll begin with his own words, written while he was stationed in Pantanella, Italy, in the summer of 1944.

1944

Twenty-Four Hours of Flight

- By Lt. Robert A. Kurb, AAF

A combat mission actually involves a full twenty-four hours — it's hard to know where it begins and where it ends. First, there's the "sweating it out," then the actual mission itself, and finally the rest and relaxation necessary after completion of the mission.

Let's start this cycle about six o'clock at night: supper is over, the bulletin board and mail tent have been checked, and you wander slowly over to Operations to see if the schedule is posted yet for the next day's raid.

Life over here is composed of many mixed emotions — what I often think of as 50-50 feelings. If you're scheduled you feel 50 percent happiness — you're glad to get another mission out of the way and be one step closer to your goal of going home; and you feel 50 percent fear or what the flight surgeon terms "apprehension" — you know from experience and observation what may happen tomorrow.

Let's assume you're scheduled. You come back to your tent, lay out your flying clothes, a fresh pack of cigarettes, some candy, put your wallet away so you won't forget and take it with you in the morning; and then settle down to write a letter to your wife. After writing and mailing the letter you amble down to the club (somehow you seem to derive a certain satisfaction in walking slowly — it promotes a feeling of calmness; it's in direct contrast to the alertness and action which will be required the next day). At the club you talk with the fellows for a few minutes, make up a sandwich, and then once more check the bulletin board at Operations to see if the schedule has changed any in the past two or three hours and also to find out what ship you're flying.

About nine o'clock you roll in and are very soon asleep — you're usually too tired to worry much at this point and experience tells you it doesn't pay anyway. From three o'clock on you sleep lightly — you're awake the minute the operations clerk steps in the tent with his flashlight and tells you the time of breakfast and briefing. You dress and wash quickly (using your canteen for the latter), blow out the candles, and go down to breakfast using your flashlight to avoid the slit trenches since it's still dark. After breakfast (where not much is said since everybody is still half asleep) you come back to the tent, gather up your things and walk over to the briefing room in the half-light of dawn. As you step in the door of the briefing hall you immediately look at the huge map at the far end of the building to find out where it's going to be today. Again you experience a 50-50 feeling — 50 percent happiness because it's going to count double, 50 percent of "uneasy stomach" because the chances are very good that it will be rougher than usual.

The briefing is a very orderly and matter-of-fact affair. You are shown your route to and from the target, where you may expect flak, what kind and how much; you are told where and when you may encounter fighters, both enemy and friendly; you're given information about the target, its value to the Axis, how it will look from your altitude, who will bomb it today, what kind of bombs will be used, how many; you're given weather information, aids to escape should you be shot or forced down in enemy territory — all of this packed intensively and logically into forty-five minutes. The briefing room is a subterranean stone hay-barn formerly used by Italian farmers in this district, and as the Chaplain comes forward to offer a prayer it is a very impressive sight, the men sitting with bowed heads in this old stone building — you feel very close to God.

After briefing there are trucks waiting outside which take you immediately to the ship. There remains about three quarters of an hour in which you assemble and check all your equipment. The guns, interphone, oxygen, the ship itself are checked thoroughly, and finally you are ready to climb aboard. You don your Mae West and over that your parachute harness; your heavier clothes and oxygen mask will be put on later at altitude, your flak suit and helmet as you near the target area.

During all this preparation you seem devoid of any particular emotions, you are busy and your mind is filled with things to be done. You may even whistle or sing as you work. The engines are started and run up, you taxi out in turn, gain the runway, and take off.

With a full gas and bomb load plus the ever-present prop wash from the ships just ahead, the take-off is packed with potential danger, but you make it all right, find your proper place in the formation, and continue in the assembly of the Group. With the assembly completed the Group, along with many similar groups, starts on course, and you're on your way.

Kicking thirty odd tons of airplane around in close formation has no parallel that I know of in civilian life. You must be alert literally every second, and the tension thus produced plus the physical fatigue evidences itself in the sweat pouring from your body.

Climbing on course you approach enemy territory, the guns are test-fired, the gunners completely equip themselves for the cold of high altitude and man their battle stations; oxygen masks and flak suits are put on, and you are ready for what may come. Before long the mask will become uncomfortable and the flak suit will feel three times its actual weight as it drags on your shoulders and rubs against the cords in your neck.

From the moment you reach enemy territory till you leave it on your way back, every man on the ship is on a straining alert, under constant tension. Outside the target area the danger lies chiefly in enemy aircraft — enemy fighters who know every trick in the game. As you scan the sky for these fighters you remember the stories you've heard, the evidences you've seen yourself of what destruction they can cause to both ships and men. If anything, this increases your vigilance; the formation tightens as if by signal because in close formation lies relative protection. Here too, you start to pray, little, short impromptu prayers that you'll be saying silently for the next three or four hours. They help immeasurably — these prayers — they give you a feeling of calmness and courage not otherwise to be found.

And so you continue on to the target, perhaps your fighter escort appears and hovers over you or flies playfully off to your side like pups frolicking on the lawn. Songs and poems have been written about those fighters, and to a bomber crew they're one of the most beautiful sights in the world — they mean protection, company and help.

Perhaps the fighters that appear aren't friendly —they're Jerries and coming in. Somehow the formation becomes even tighter, gunners call them off around the clock — "There's two of them high at three o'clock movin' around to four. You've got 'em, Dave." You sit there tensely as you hear the guns chatter, you wait for the answering "smacks" as the enemy tracers find your ship but this time he doesn't get you. Dave got one and scared the other away. You wish you had the power to award medals — he'd get the Congressional Medal right now! You wet your lips and once again start to scan the sky.

Now you're approaching the target area; you brace yourself inwardly, your prayers are more frequent, the tension in the whole ship mounts, you even sense it in the engines. This is where you're going to get flak — you hope you won't feel it but you'll see it — dirty black puffs like miniature clouds; it'll be everywhere, you'll see a solid wall of it ahead, above, below, everywhere. You can't get through it again — it's impossible. You've seen it knock ships out of the air, you've seen it wound and kill men, you've seen crews bail out over the target, their chutes drifting hopelessly down into the black smoke many thousands of feet below. Every time it happens — you know the law of averages — maybe today it'll be you instead of those other fellows.

With a completely empty feeling in your stomach you clamp on your flak helmet and start to ride it through. You're watching the instruments, the formation, the flak, you feel those ragged pieces of steel tear into the ship, you wonder if it was the ship only that was hit, you haven't time to pray, you hear "bombs away," and still you're in it — seconds like hours, minutes almost days. The ship lurches and bucks through the sky as it's tossed around by hits and near-hits, all you can see is flak; then finally the turn, a minute more, and it's all over.

At least there's no more flak, there may still be fighters, but somehow right now you're too relieved to worry. You feel awfully good, you feel great, life is wonderful!

The minute you leave the target area a check is immediately made on the men and the ship. Can you make it back, what's been hit, gas leaks, engines feathered, hydraulic system shot out? Are any of the men hurt, give them first aid, make them comfortable, and hurry.

You fly on a few minutes; the check is completed, maybe you have only three engines, but you're still flying and you're still in formation. Everybody starts to chatter at once — "You should see the hole back here in the waist, missed my foot by about six inches; there goes a B-24 down — 4, 6, 8, 10 chutes, it's OK, everybody got out," and so on. The ball gunner says you plastered the target and everybody grins — it's a long hard trip to make and you don't want to make it again.

Now you're coming home and everybody's spirits are rising. There's more talk on the interphone, but everyone remains alert and the formation stays tight. At last you reach friendly territory, flak suits, oxygen masks are ripped off, you light up a cigarette that tastes better than any you've ever had in your life, and the world becomes a wonderful place again.

You continue on back to the base, peel off, and land. Trucks once more await you and you're taken immediately to interrogation (the briefing room of the morning). Before going down you get the coffee and doughnut line. Here everyone is talking at once and usually in a loud voice — somehow it helps to relieve that tension accumulated during the last seven or eight hours. As you hungrily gulp the "coffee and" you feel yourself letting down, relaxing; and with the relaxation comes a stupor-like weariness.

You force yourself to remain alert during interrogation as you tell the intelligence officer everything you saw today — fighters, flak, results of bombing, ships shot down, etc. With interrogation finished you walk back to the tent, dead tired, hot dirty and hungry, but you have a good feeling inside of a job well done and the knowledge that you made it back once again. You flop down on your cot and in a few minutes are trying to gain enough ambition to make it to the shower. Sometimes you do, sometimes you don't, you really don't care much.

In a couple of hours it's time for supper and the cycle starts again. Perhaps you're up tomorrow, at any rate you're one step closer to going home and that thought gives you sufficient satisfaction for the present. You amble slowly down to the mess hall wondering whether there will be a letter for you tonight.

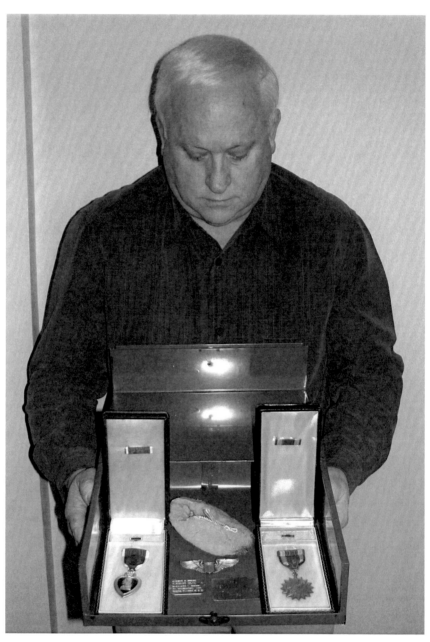

Jim Kurtz with several items he discovered in the green box

THE GREEN BOX

I T WAS THE SUMMER OF 1957, A TYPICALLY OPPRESSIVE "DOG day" in August. I had just celebrated my eighth birthday. Life was mostly good.

My mom, my three brothers, and I lived at 9 Ralph Avenue, in White Plains, New York, a cozy, comfortable suburb about 30 miles north of New York City. When he was alive, my dad had commuted into Manhattan and my mom would pile us four boys into the car and drive to the train station to meet him. I don't remember that or anything else about my dad. One cold March day, when I was almost three years old, he had died of a massive heart attack. Life at our home would never be the same. My mother was devastated by the loss of her husband. In one moment she had become a 30-year-old single mom of four boys, ages two through nine.

I don't remember much about the first eight years of my life, but I know I always felt deeply loved, not only by my mom, but by my three older brothers as well. We were bonded forever by the loss of our father. A tightly knit family, the Kurtzes depended on each other; it is how we pulled through. One thing I do remember distinctly about the early years of my life was the lack of any discussion about my father. Concern for our mother's grief was paramount, and we knew not to mention his name or ask questions about him. I was over 50 years old before I had my first conversation with my mother about my dad.

As a young boy, most of what I learned about my father was a result of eavesdropping. Stories were told about Dad being a pilot in the big war a few years earlier, somewhere far away in a place called Europe. When the adults would gather to chat in the living room, I would play inconspicuously on the floor in the next room, listening intently, drinking in every word and trying to make whatever sense I could of their discussion. I heard horrible stories about a plane crash, POW camps, and starvation. I remember feeling an overwhelming sadness and shock when I realized it was my father they were talking about. Although I never really knew him, it was incomprehensible to me that anyone would want to hurt my dad. The adults would also talk about strange numbers and letters like B-24, and even stranger names like Liberator. I knew my father had been a bomber pilot, but had never realized a bomber and a B-24 Liberator were one and the same. I wondered if all these stories I had overheard could somehow be related to the green box I had seen in the attic when I was younger. I was unaware of it at the time, but the next 56 years of my life were to be defined by its contents. My quest to find out about this wonderful man, the father I never knew, was about to begin.

It was a steamy late summer's afternoon; I had just turned eight and realized I could wait no longer to discover what was in the green box. I needed a time when all three of my brothers were not home. It was an unspoken rule that the box and its contents were off limits and I couldn't take the chance that one of them would tell my mom what I was planning to do. I could hear my mother vacuuming downstairs as I grabbed a flashlight and silently crept up to the attic.

I opened the door and was met by a blast of heat; it must have been close to 100 degrees up there, but that wasn't going to stop me. It took a couple of seconds for my eyes to adjust to the darkness and as I waited impatiently, I worried that my mother would soon come looking for me. Every second was important. I stood there squinting as objects began to take shape and then suddenly, there it was— the green metal box that I knew had been my father's. About nine inches long and four inches tall and olive drab, it was sitting on the shelf of an old yellow bookcase. Until that day, I had never gathered up enough courage to actually touch it, let alone open it. That moment is still etched in my mind. I sat on the floor drenched in sweat. The fear of getting caught, and therefore punished, was very real, and yet I had to find out what magical and mysterious contents this army-green box had to offer. I knew I didn't have much time.

I nervously opened the lid and the first thing revealed by the beam of my flashlight was an array of colors: reds, silvers, yellows, greens, and a particularly striking purple. I would find out years later that they were the ribbons my dad had earned and worn on his dress uniform. There were also two navy-blue boxes with the words "Air Medal" on one and "Purple Heart" on the other. I looked at the Air Medal box first. Slowly, with a lump forming in my throat, I opened it. The ribbon was a stunning blue and orange that mesmerized me. On the face of the medal was an eagle with a fierce expression; its talons held lightning bolts. Although I didn't know what it was or why he had it, I could tell it was my dad's, because inscribed on the back was "2nd Lt. Robert R. Kurtz AC." As I touched every detail of the medal, the tips of my fingers felt as if they were burning. It made me feel intensely proud of my father. I would learn more about the Air Medal at a later date.

The Purple Heart box was next. I opened it and found a purple-and-white ribbon attached to a heart-shaped medal. It was gold on the outside with a purple interior and a silhouette of George Washington in the center. I was spellbound. On the reverse side, in raised gold lettering, were the words "For Military Merit," and etched below, "Robert R. Kurtz." For this too, it would be years before I learned its significance: an award given to soldiers wounded during military service.

Time was running short, but there were so many more items in the box. One that caught my eye was a pink fluffy baby slipper that zippered up the front. Everything I had seen so far had been military in nature. Medals, ribbons, silver wings, and gold bars were all obviously a part of my father's life during his World War II service. Why would there be a baby slipper among these items?

Right before closing the lid, I noticed a bundle of papers. Several bore the bold stamp of Western Union; I had never seen a telegram before. There were official-looking documents from the Army Air Force and letters from my father to my mom and to his parents. There were also papers with my father's picture on the front and his fingerprints on the back surrounded by writing in a strange language that I had never seen. Years later, I found out they were prisoner of war identification forms; the language was German.

My time was up, at least for the day. A whole new world had opened up to me. I had so many questions, some of which would not be answered for years, but one thing was undeniable. As I closed the box, I knew my life had been changed forever.

AND SO IT ALL BEGAN

I T WAS APRIL 20, 1941, AND WHAT HAD BEEN A BITTERLY COLD, snowy winter was finally letting up. A stiff breeze was blowing and as my mom looked up at the tree branches, she was glad to see red and green buds beginning to appear on the bare limbs, a sure sign that spring couldn't be far away. For the first time in months, she felt the sun's warmth on her face and it lifted her spirits. The break in the weather, which had made the day so wonderful, had her feeling lighthearted. Although she couldn't put her finger on it, she sensed that something different and special might happen to her soon. She would be 20 years old in May, the country was on the verge of war, and my mom had no idea what the future would bring. But at least for that day, she decided to put her worries aside and enjoy herself.

She was on her way to a music program at the Church in the Highlands, within walking distance of her home in White Plains. Normally, her best friend, Edith, would have joined her, but on this particular Sunday afternoon, Edith had family plans. My mom was hoping that another one of her girlfriends might be there, but upon entering the church and realizing she was early, she took a seat at the far end of a pew. Out of the corner of her eye, she spotted someone moving towards her and smiled, thinking that one of the girls must have decided to come after all. When she looked up to see who it was, she was met by the warmest pair of hazel green eyes she had ever seen. They belonged to a handsome, brown-haired young man and she found herself blushing. My mother would never forget the next words spoken to her: "Hi, my name's Bob Kurtz. If you're not expecting anyone to join you, would you mind if I sat here?" That man was my father. Decades later, in a letter she wrote to all of her grandchildren, my mom described the moment she met my dad in a simple, but life-changing phrase: "and so it all began."

Robert Russell Kurtz, the son of Russell and Persis Kurtz, was born in Akron, Ohio, on January 8, 1919. He and his sister, Katherine, lived there with their parents until they moved to White Plains, New

York, in 1933. He entered the local high school in September, graduating in the spring of 1936. That fall, he attended Bowdoin College in Maine, but after a year decided to return to White Plains to live at home and continue his education at the New York University School of Commerce in Manhattan, which he attended until his induction into the Army.

Margaret "Peggy" Florence Luther was born in Cleveland, Ohio, on May 19, 1921, where she lived with her parents, Ward and Florence, her sister, Helen, and her brother, Ward, until she was seven years old. Although the Great Depression was still officially a year away, the company her father worked for fell on hard times and was forced to let him go. Fortunately, my mother's Aunt Lettie owned a successful lingerie company in New York City that sold to markets in Europe. Concerned about her sister's family, she offered Ward a job as manager and within weeks, the Luther family moved to White Plains, where they would live for the rest of their lives.

My mom always enjoyed telling me about her childhood years. She lived in a middle-class area of White Plains known as the Highlands that included an abundance of starter homes with young families. She made a lot of friends and those early relationships lasted a lifetime. In her 2000 letter to her grandchildren, she wrote: "Those were happy years for me. We lived in a neighborhood with many kids, boys and girls, and we had such good times. To this day, at 78 years old, I still hear from and see some of them, which is amazing."

Pictures of my mother as a teenager show a beautiful young woman. She was very popular and was elected president of her high school sorority her senior year. Hours a day were spent on outdoor activities: bike riding, sailing, roller skating, ice skating, or just taking walks. Above all, she loved to dance. As sorority president, my mother organized dances at nearby country clubs. One of her favorite memories was dancing with her high school sweetheart at the Glen Island Casino in New Rochelle where Benny Goodman and his band were playing live. Mom always said she was a one-man girl. "I went with the same boy through high school and one year of college, and then Bob for the rest of his life."

After graduating from White Plains High School in 1939, my mother went to Sweet Briar College in Virginia, but after one year decided it wasn't for her. She was an intelligent woman and had

Bob Kurtz in front of the White Plains train station, Spring 1939

always gotten good grades, so her father insisted that she pursue a career. She chose to attend Katherine Gibbs Secretarial School in New York City, moving back home and commuting daily to school. Coincidentally, Bob Kurtz was also riding the train to New York every day. Edith told me 70 years later that she had a secret crush on my father and often sat with him on the train and on car rides home. But my dad only had eyes for one girl, admiring her from afar until he got up the nerve to sit next to her that Sunday afternoon in church. According to Edith, "Your dad offered me a ride home from the train station the Monday after he had met your mom, except this time, she was there too. She jumped into the front seat next to your father and I never sat there again."

My father was drafted in the spring of 1941, but was allowed to defer induction until July so that he could finish his school year at NYU. What followed were three wonderful and exciting months for my parents as they got to know each other and fall in love. Almost every day, my dad would pick up my mom at the train station and they would drive over to Larchmont, a beautiful shore town not far from White Plains. They would walk, hand in hand, out to a gazebo that overlooked Long Island Sound, hoping to view another glorious sunset, or just sit in his car and, as my mother remembered, "talk and talk."

In May, my mother graduated from Katherine Gibbs and began to look for a job. My father, knowing that he would have to report for duty in a couple of months, made plans to go back to Carey, Ohio, with his mother to see close relatives. My mom always smiled when

she told me what happened next: "His birthday present to me was a train trip to meet him in Cleveland. Much to my surprise, my parents let me go; I guess it was because of the war getting closer."

When she returned home, my mother got a job as secretary to the vice president of Citizens Bank, spending every non-working moment with my father. They were inseparable. My mother told me that "we just enjoyed being together no matter what we were doing." They only had two months left before his induction, and they made every minute count. Movies, bike rides, walks on the beach, and car rides to nowhere filled their nights and weekends. They talked constantly, taking turns describing their childhood years. They marveled at the coincidences of their youth: they both had been born in Ohio to strict but loving parents, and both had moved to White Plains with their families due to worsening economic times. They did not see their

My parents enjoying quiet moments during their chaperoned courtship before my father's induction, Cape Cod, 1941

shared commute as a random circumstance; rather they believed it was fate, plain and simple, a sign that their relationship was meant to be.

On July 23, 1941, my father was inducted into the United States Army at Fort Jay, Governor's Island, New York, and was immediately assigned to the United States Army Coastal Artillery Unit at Camp Davis in Holly Ridge, North Carolina, where he trained for close to a year. My mother stayed in White Plains and continued to work as a secretary. She and my father wrote to each other almost every day; being apart was maddening, but the intensity of how much they missed each other made them realize how much in love they were.

My father in 1941 after his induction, wearing his newly issued uniform. Perhaps he chose the location for this photo as a subtle comment on Army food.

With the country preparing for war and the men under a rigorous training schedule, few furloughs were granted. All my parents had were their letters and an occasional phone call.

Although he was training to be a soldier in an artillery unit, my father's dream had always been to be a pilot, so he volunteered to be an aviation cadet and was placed in the Air Corps unassigned pool. He knew that when the United States went to war there would be an enormous need for manpower in all sectors of the military, and he hoped he would eventually be accepted into flight training.

Camp Davis was typical of many other military training facilities that sprang up around the country. Construction of the base began in December of 1940, providing hundreds of jobs for locals and turning the sleepy town of Holly Ridge into a bustling military city.[1] The first batch of 28,000 recruits arrived in April of 1941. The war began in earnest for the United States in December of that year; each month, thousands of men and women were drafted or enlisted. Training camps such as Davis expanded dramatically, and in 1943, its population had ballooned to an incredible 110,000 people![2]

By December of 1941, my father was in the best physical shape of his life, but emotionally, he was hurting. He had been away from my mother for more than five months. Troubling news of German advances in Europe weighed heavily on all the soldiers' minds. The intensity of their training had heightened, and almost all of the men assumed that the Unites States would be entering the war sooner rather than later. Their assumptions were confirmed within a week. On December 7, 1941, the Empire of Japan attacked the United States Naval Yard at Pearl Harbor in Hawaii, killing and wounding thousands of American sailors. The next day, President Franklin Roosevelt addressed Congress, expressing his outrage over the surprise attack, proclaiming December 7, 1941, as "a date which will live in infamy." His speech was heard by millions of stunned Americans sitting around their home radios; the war that most had hoped to avoid was now upon them.

One of my favorite things to do as a child was to go up to the attic and read every telegram in the green box. I must have read them scores of times. They took on more meaning as I matured and continued my education, but there was one that puzzled me for years. I couldn't ask my mother because that box was supposed to be off limits. It was wired to her from Camp Davis and read:

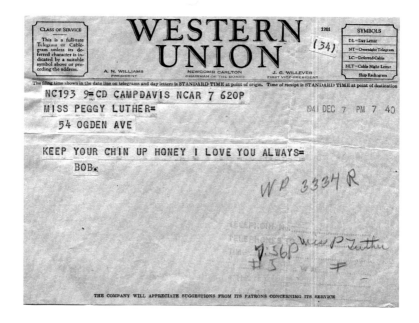

When I began to write this book, I read all the telegrams again and when I came across that one, it finally made sense: the date of the telegram was December 7, 1941.

On December 8, the United States declared war on Japan. Three days later, Germany and Italy entered into the conflict by declaring war on the United States, which had no choice but to reciprocate in what was now a full-fledged global war. With the war effort in full swing, physical training at Camp Davis was ramped up. Sit-ups, push-ups, crunches, and chin-ups were all part of daily routines used to build up muscles that were sure to be called on during warfare. My father was thankful for the cooler December air, especially during calisthenics, as the brutally hot North Carolina summer months had made it difficult even to breathe through the grueling exercises. My dad trained hard, knowing that pilots in the United States Army Air Corps (which would become the Army Air Force in March of 1942) had to be in perfect physical condition. Unlike modern aircraft with controls that respond to the lightest touch, the heavy bombers of World War II required intense upper body strength to steer. He didn't know yet if he would make it into the Air Corps, but as the war began to ramp up, he was glad that he was fit.

Carrying on a long-distance relationship with my mother was difficult, but their love for each other was strong, as epitomized by this wire he sent her on January 30, 1942:

HOPE YOU'RE VERY HAPPY TONIGHT DEAREST.
WISH I COULD BE WITH YOU. I LOVE YOU WITH
ALL MY HEART FOREVER, BOB.

A few weeks later, my dad's hopes of becoming a pilot were partially realized when he was selected for pilot training. He would still have to complete extensive flight instruction on the ground, as well as demanding fitness regimens, before he could begin aviation cadet school. But he was one step closer to his dream.

In the meantime, granted a short leave, he grabbed the chance to go home to see my mother. Not knowing when the call back to duty would come, my parents decided to get married right away. As was true for so many wartime couples, they had to move quickly. In her 2000 letter, my mom recalled how pressed they were for time. "We had a week to have all tests and make necessary arrangements. We were married on March 28, 1942, at my home on Ogden Avenue with twenty-one dollars a month, and my small salary, but where there's a will, there's a way." Although she glossed over the details of her wedding in the letter to her grandchildren, the contents of the green box provided further information. The ceremony was at 8:00 p.m. on a Saturday night at my mother's parents' home. A quiet gathering of 20-30 relatives and friends witnessed the vows performed by the Reverend Arthur S. Wheelock, minister of the Church in the Highlands, where my parents had first met. A short reception followed, and the next morning they were off to Boston for a one-week honeymoon. They returned to find that my dad had been ordered back to Camp Davis. The next morning, the newlyweds reluctantly said their goodbyes and my father headed back down south.

My dad had been in North Carolina for only a couple of days when he found out there would be a delay in reporting to aviation cadet school due to a backup in flight training in the USAAF. Because there was no reason for further artillery training at Camp Davis, he applied for leave. The Army's response triggered this emotional telegram to my mom on April 8:

WILL KNOW THURSDAY ABOUT POSSIBILITY
OF 90 DAY FURLOUGH SUBJECT TO 24 HOUR
RECALL. PLEASE DON'T GET YOUR HOPES TOO
HIGH DARLING. I LOVE YOU, BOB.

Upon receiving it, my mother was beside herself with joy, only to
have her hopes dashed the next day:

FURLOUGH DELAYED. DECISION SATURDAY.
HOLD TIGHT, LOVE, BOB.

The wonderful news arrived Sunday: my father had been granted
the furlough and was on his way home. My mother described the

Newlyweds Bob and Peggy, 1942

next two months in one sentence: "We rented a third floor apartment in a house in White Plains and lived as if we had a lifetime ahead of us." Time flew by with the two of them "making every second count."

On June 15, orders came to return to Camp Davis, the furlough having been cut short by a few weeks. Even though they knew it was coming, the news was heartwrenching. With war raging in both Europe and the Pacific, listings of dead and wounded American soldiers appeared every day in the local paper. Now and then, they recognized names of boys from their high school who had been killed in action; it was sobering news, striking fear in their hearts. But my father was no different than any other American soldier—patriotic and proud to defend his country. The next day, although neither one of them wanted to let the other go, my parents parted and my father was once again on his way back to Camp Davis.

On June 20, the Commanding General at Camp Davis issued a letter to my father and four other soldiers, ordering them to proceed to an Army Air Force Aviation Cadet School in Sacramento, California. The directives were simple and precise:

```
Travel by rail on June 23, 1942. Proceed
to Mather Field, Sacramento, California.
The Quartermaster will issue 13 party
meal tickets at the rate not to exceed
$1.00 per meal when meals are taken in
dining car on railroad train, or at the
rate of not to exceed $0.75 per meal when
meals are taken elsewhere. By order and
command of Major General Smith.[3]
```

Three days later, my dad boarded a train for California. He was entering an exciting new chapter of his life and couldn't stop thinking, "I'm finally getting what I've always wanted. I'm going to be a pilot!"

For the first few months at Mather Field, the new cadet was primarily in classroom instruction or enduring exercise regimens equal to or harder than those at Camp Davis. Training 16-18 hours per day was not unusual and the aviation cadets were exhausted all the time. One evening in July, my father decided to lie down on his cot for a badly needed breather when he was told there was a phone call from home. It was my mom, and her news sent him into a state of euphoria. She was pregnant! After talking to her for a few minutes, making sure she was feeling all right, he hung up and rushed back to his barracks to spread the news. There were handshakes and back-slapping galore and he loved every second of it. When things finally quieted down, he went to see his commanding officer and asked for a furlough. A fifteen-day leave was all they could offer him. At first, he thought it would be impossible to travel the entire country and back in that amount of time, but the more he thought about it, the more determined he became. Traveling by rail was too expensive. Besides, in 1942, most trains were transporting troops and were overcrowded and slow to reach their destination. That left just one option—his thumb. The next morning, he began a cross-country hitchhiking od-yssey that defied all odds. It started off slowly, but somewhere in the middle of New Mexico, he caught his big break—a trucker offered him a long-distance ride. After crossing the border into Texas, he went to the Western Union office in Amarillo, and wired this mes-sage to my mother:

> HAVE A SWELL RIDE FROM NEW MEXICO THROUGH TO COLUMBUS OHIO. WILL PROBABLY GET HOME MONDAY. I LOVE YOU, DARLING, BOB.

He was in White Plains two days later.

He was only able to see my mother for a few days and they shared their good news with anyone who would listen. Before they knew it, my dad had to hit the road and, once again, they were saying their goodbyes. But this time, my mom was not as sad as she had been previously. Even though her husband was hitchhiking back to Cali-fornia, she was carrying his child, and thus a part of him would stay with her—a thought that brought her immense comfort.

Amazingly, my father made it back to Sacramento on the last day of his furlough. Overwhelmed and inspired by the kindness of all the men and women who had stopped to pick him up, he sent a letter and short essay about his cross-country journey to the local newspaper. It was so well received that it was forwarded to a national magazine, *The Atlantic Monthly*, and published the following month. An editor supplied the introduction for his piece: "I have said that you feel the rising spirit of the country. To show what I mean, I have cut out this letter of a young aviator, Robert R. Kurtz, which appeared in the *Inglewood Daily News:*"

> I've just returned from a 15-day furlough and a very interesting 7,000-mile trip. Stationed in California and living just outside of New York City, I found myself faced with the prospect of hitchhiking coast-to-coast and back or not going home at all. Since my wife was soon to have a baby, the decision was not a hard one to make although I had never hit the road before.
>
> I reached home in four days—100 hours to be exact—but it's not the speed of my trip that was important. Rather it was the spirit, the friendliness of all those American people who picked me up, who went out of their way time and time again, who always left me with a smiling, "Good luck, soldier." I've been in the Army a year now and have heard many a "beef" from soldiers regarding the attitude of civilians toward the men in service. This may be true in some communities, but I can certainly attest that it is not true of the country as a whole.
>
> Why should a farmer's wife carry me ten miles out of her way in order that I might more easily get a ride at an important junction; what prompted a Harrisburg salesman and his wife to spend fifteen minutes unloading their back seat of luggage and clothes so that I might find room to stretch out and sleep; why did families always insist on buying my meals when we stopped for something to eat? When I protested, their answer was always the same: "You boys are doing a lot for us, aren't you? This is the least we can do for you." That "least" is something I'll never forget as long as I live; from New York to California I found it everywhere. An Iowa farmer, a Pittsburgh banker, a Wyoming rancher, a New Jersey defense worker—all of them going out of their way for a boy in uniform, all of them modestly telling me how they were doing their part on the home front.

The editor concluded: "The author is an aviation cadet, aged twenty-three, now stationed in California. Good writing, soldier!"[4]

My father remained at Mather Field until late 1942. He was champing at the bit to get behind the controls of a plane, but still had not been given official notification of acceptance for pilot training. In late October, my mother received a letter from W.A. Robertson, Colonel, Army Air Forces, Commanding. Dated 19 October, 1942; it read:

> Dear Mrs. Kurtz, It is with great pleasure that I notify you that your husband, Robert R. Kurtz has been selected by the Classification Board for Pilot training in the United States Army Air Forces. I congratulate you both on this achievement. He will soon be transferred to one of the West Coast Army Air Force Training Center elementary flying schools and will then begin his flight training.

Col. Robertson's words make clear why my father wanted to be a pilot:

> In either war or peace, a Pilot occupies a position that requires sound judgment, a keen and alert mind, a sound body and the ability to perfectly coordinate mind and body in the flying of the airplane. It is imperative that the men who fly our military aircraft possess these qualifications, for upon their skill will depend in large measure the success of our war effort.
>
> It is my hope that you will derive great satisfaction from your husband's selection for Pilot training, and that his future career in the Army Air Forces will be one of continuing success and service.[5]

In December, my father was assigned to a USAAF Aviation Cadet School in Ontario, California. He began his initial flight training on a PT-13B Kaydet biplane. Built by Boeing-Stearman, it was the primary trainer for USAAF pilots.[6] Both student and instructor sat in an open cockpit, one in front of the other. The first time at the controls gave my father an adrenaline rush like none he had ever experienced before. Flying in the "wild blue yonder" was exhilarating, but at the same time, frightening as hell! My dad flew every day and after a couple of weeks, he was logging solo time. He became more and more comfortable in the cockpit. He relished the feeling of being in control and now there was no question in his mind: his decision to become a pilot had been the right one.

I found records of every hour of my dad's Ontario PT-13B flight times in the green box, as well as all the hours he had logged at the five USAAF bases that were to follow, as he prepared to ship overseas. He was stationed at Ontario from December of 1942 through February of 1943. During that time, he logged 35:50 hours of dual time and 24:10 solo time, giving him a total of 60 hours in the air.

In late February, my father was transferred to War Eagle Field, a USAAF base in Lancaster, California, where he learned maneuvers on a BT-15 Valiant, another single-engine plane with a solid reputation as a quality trainer for aviation cadets.[7] He had trouble concentrating from the moment he got to Lancaster—not necessarily a good thing when you are just learning to fly planes, but understandable given that my mother was due any day. When he thought he couldn't stand the suspense another minute, he received the call he had been waiting for. His mother called with the news that Peggy was fine, having just given birth to a healthy seven-and-a-half pound baby boy, my oldest brother, Robert Russell Kurtz, Jr. After asking dozens of detailed questions, he hung up and then it really hit him. As the wonderful news sank in, my dad couldn't stop smiling and thinking to himself, "I have a son. I have a son!"

After sharing his joy with everyone who was within earshot, he sat down and wrote my mother the most romantic letter I have ever read. The correspondence and telegrams in the green box have helped me to understand what type of man my father was; they have given me insights into both his personal and military life. But the letter he penned to my mother that Saturday night in early March, 1943, stands out above all the rest. It was still in its original envelope, marked special delivery and addressed to Mrs. Robert R. Kurtz, White Plains Hospital. Even when I was eight years old and didn't fully understand what I was reading, I knew it was beautiful. As a teenager, when I began dating and fell in love every other week, I would sneak up to the attic to reread his letter. My dad's profession of love for her was inspiring. Fifty years later, I asked my mother why she had never remarried or at least thought about it. Her reply was, "I had already met the man of my life. No one could have replaced him."

My own very, very precious wife, Oh baby dearest, I'm so very proud and happy tonight. I've just been walking around with a grin on my face ever since Mother called! Darling, it was Bobby, wasn't it, we've been talking about our baby always as "he" and now our dreams have all come true, just think, our own precious baby son, I'm so happy!! ... Was it awfully painful, honey, you've been so very brave and uncomplaining thru all these months. I hope and pray that Bobby wasn't too difficult about making his appearance. If you only knew how I've been thinking of you dearest, I was so relieved to hear that both you and the baby were fine. Even though I haven't been sleeping as much, I've been sticking to my job, sweetheart, so please don't worry on that score, it just wasn't possible to go to sleep every night as if nothing was happening ... When I got Mother's call, I would have given anything to talk to you. When you get home from the hospital I'll call you, darling, and maybe we can time it so that Bobby can say hello too or at least cry it. Oh sweetheart, if I could only be there with you to see him, to tell and show you how very happy and proud I am, I worship you, my baby, and adore you with all of me! ... Oh honey, just think, we have a son, a precious little baby all our own, I'll bet he's the most perfect baby ever born cause he's certainly got the most perfect mother in all the world! ... Gee, honey, I never knew I had so many friends before, word spread all over the post in half an hour and supper tonight was one long celebration, fellows kept coming up all thru the meal offering their congratulations and slapping me on the back, it was just like our wedding night and I was so happy and proud. The three fellows whose wives have had babies before ours all had girls so I was the envy of them all ... Do you mind too much if I had a cigar tonight, sweetheart, I just had to celebrate in some way, oh dearest, I'm so proud and happy! ... In just a couple of months you and Bobby will be here with me and then everything will be completely perfect, oh darling, I can't wait for you to come, to hold you both close in my arms, it'll be heaven! Goodnight, my beloved, I'll dream of you and Bobby all night, I worship you both more than I can ever tell you. Your very own, Bob.

By Monday, the excitement had subsided somewhat; my dad was flying again, and it was back to business as usual. My parents wrote each other almost every day and, when he had the chance, they would talk on the phone. She loved to give him day-to-day updates of what their new baby was up to. They knew my dad was going to be transferred to an advanced training base fairly soon. Families were allowed to join the soldiers at that time; the problem was that they didn't know where they would be going. For the next two months, my father continued flying the BT-15 and by the beginning of April, he had accumulated another 70 hours in the air. In Ontario, he had logged more dual time than solo time, but as he became more experienced, the ratios changed. At War Eagle Field, he flew 40 solo hours and 30 dual. On April 10, 1943, he received orders to report to the Marfa Army Air Forces Advanced Flying School at the Marfa Air Base, in Marfa, Texas. He had put in more than 130 hours in the air.

In March of 1942, the War Department chose Marfa as a site for training USAAF advanced twin-engine pilots.[8] Located in west Texas, 200 miles southeast of El Paso, it was a perfect location for an air base, sparsely populated and surrounded by desert. Construction began in June of 1942, and soon, six 7,500-foot asphalt runways had been completed.[9] A hospital, mess hall, chapel, theater, army barracks, hangars, and a control tower were built simultaneously. By the time my father arrived, Marfa Air Base was buzzing with activity.

Stories of the stifling summer temperatures in western Texas were legendary, and although it was only early April, the heat was already oppressive. Rigorous physical training was still an essential part of cadet life, and the hospital on base was constantly treating men for dehydration. Flight training was intensified and they were in the air all the time. AT-17B Bobcats, manufactured by Cessna and nicknamed "Bamboo Bombers," were the advanced trainer aircraft used to bridge the gap between single-engine trainers and twin-engine aircraft. The cockpit consisted of two flight control positions, the left side for the pilot and the right for the co-pilot. Although much smaller in size, it partially resembled the cockpit of the B-24 Liberators they would be flying in the near future.[10] Flight logs were kept differently at Marfa Air Base. Besides dual and solo hours, my father accumulated valuable co-pilot flight time, hours he would need to graduate and receive his wings.

Although flight training required attention to detail and uninterrupted focus on the job at hand, my father's thoughts were never far from his wife and baby. He had been looking for lodging for them since the day he arrived. On April 22, 1943, my dad sent a telegram with the good news. He must have been so excited that he was unable to wait another minute to send her the wire. Western Union stamped the hour as 4:16 a.m. and it read:

> HAVE WONDERFUL SETUP RESERVED FOR ABOUT MAY 23RD. WILL WRITE YOU IN DETAIL TONIGHT. THIS IS OUR BREAK HONEY. I ADORE YOU. BOB.

They had their hands full, my father with training and my mother with Bobby. Despite these time-consuming tasks, the next four weeks dragged on endlessly as my parents anticipated the first time all three of them would be together, and the moment my dad would finally hold his son.

An article I found in the green box had appeared in the local White Plains newspaper, *The Reporter Dispatch*, in May of 1943. My grandfather had supplied the information:

> KURTZES GO TO TEXAS. Mrs. Robert R. Kurtz and her infant son, Robert R. Kurtz, Jr., left last night for Indian Lodge, Fort Davis, Tex., where Aviation Cadet Kurtz is stationed. They were accompanied by Mrs. Russell Kurtz of Hartsdale Gardens Apartments, who will remain with her son and his family until he receives his wings June 22. The senior Mrs. Kurtz will

return to White Plains at that time and her daughter-in-law and grandson will remain in Texas.[11]

My mother understatedly described the train trip from White Plains to Texas as "rough." My brother was only three months old and there was no air conditioning in the overcrowded rail cars. The train was filled with troops on their way to new assignments, so civilian travel was not a priority. My mother told me years later that, without exception, the soldiers were polite and did their best to make her and Bobby as comfortable as possible, even if it meant giving up their seat so they could lie down. In subsequent train travel, as my mom and brother followed my dad from air base to air base, the same held true. She would always remember how accommodating the men in uniform had been.

The last few hours on the train before they arrived in Marfa were anxious ones. My mother had not seen my father for ten months and she counted off the minutes as they drew near the railroad station. She had imagined the moment a thousand times when Bob would first see the face of their little boy. She wanted to hold her husband in her arms and never let go. The screeching of the train brakes startled her and she looked out the window, realizing they were in Marfa. Aviation cadets were lined up on the platform and she was hoping my father had been able to get an hour or two off from training to meet them. Although drained from the long trip, my grandmother did the best she could to help, holding my wiggling brother while her daughter-in-law struggled with their luggage. My mom scanned the excited crowd looking for any sign of her husband. All of a sudden, there he was. From that point on, it was all a blur of emotional hugs and kisses; they were back together once again.

For the next month, my mother, brother, and grandmother stayed right outside the base at Indian Lodge, a rustic one-level stone structure in Fort Davis, Texas, that my mother amusingly called in her 2000 letter, "sort of a resort." She also wrote that "he was able to get off at times to be with us" but, for the most part, nearly every hour of his day involved flight or classroom training. Graduation was rapidly approaching and the aviation cadets needed to complete the required flight hours necessary to get their wings and become pilots. The time my father got to spend with his family meant everything to him, but my mother could clearly see he was exhausted. By June 21, my dad had logged 23:20 dual, 50:30 solo, and 58:40 co-pilot hours of flight time.

The next day was graduation for the class of 43-F. A letter from the public relations office at Marfa Air Base sent to relatives that were unable to attend the ceremony best describes what my mother witnessed the morning of June 22:

> An impressive aerial demonstration---
> the first to be given on the field---
> featured Tuesday's graduation exercises
> at the Advanced Flying School, where
> young men from forty states received
> wings, second lieutenant's commissions,
> and a message of cheer and confidence
> for their coming jobs in the cause of
> freedom. Starting promptly at nine A.M.,
> sixty cadets, who lacked but an hour of
> being full-fledged officers, flew over the
> landing field in thirty-six twin engine
> training ships, maintaining a perfect
> formation. Dividing into two groups at
> the end of the runway, they made right
> and left turns respectively; then met
> again at the opposite end to form a new
> pattern and thrill spectators with their
> continued precision. None of the usual
> crowd that thronged the flying line could
> have entertained any doubts that the new
> pilots were in the peak of condition---
> that their training had borne fruit in the
> form of expert airmanship. Friends and
> relatives strained their necks and eyes
> as the planes roared overhead, sharply
> outlined against a sky of cloudless blue.

More than 50 years later, my mother recalled how proud she felt as the cadets' planes soared over the airfield, the cacophony deafening as they buzzed the awestruck crowd. After the air demonstration, everyone entered the Base Theater, where Commanding Officer Colonel Hoyle presented wings and commissions to the graduates. The guest speaker was Lt. Paul E. Ray, who had flown B-26 medium bombers in the Pacific Theater and had been awarded the Silver Star and Distinguished Flying Cross for his actions. Addressing family and friends, Ray assured them that their boys would be flying the world's best and safest aircraft. He stated, "The enemy's planes have proven good, but ours have proven better. Furthermore, our boys will always receive the best of medical attention, wherever they are. Simultaneously, with the establishment of a base is always the establishment of a well-equipped hospital." Turning his attention to the new graduates, he said, "Every new situation in combat will be different, but you new pilots have the training to cope with it." He ended his speech by congratulating the newly commissioned second lieutenants for their hard work and wishing them well for whatever the future would hold.

The final sentence from the public relations letter provides a lasting image:

> Holding his wings and commission, the graduate awaited only a kiss from the hometown sweetheart and the first salute from an enlisted man to feel like a full-fledged officer ready for heavy responsibility.[12]

After graduation, my grandmother returned to White Plains, while my mother packed up for my father's next transfer to the USAAF base in Moses Lake, Washington. A couple of days later, the young family boarded the train in Marfa for their long journey northward. Conditions in the railway cars mirrored those on her trip to Texas, but now the soaring hundred-degree temperatures were exacerbated by increased humidity, making breathing almost impossible. My mother told me, "A couple of soldiers gave up their sleeping compartment to your dad and me, so that we could give Bobby a place to sleep. I don't know what I would have done without your father there."

Once they reached Washington, my mother and Bobby got off at Wenatchee, about 70 miles from Moses Lake Air Base. She found temporary lodging and awaited word about housing near the airfield. Before they even had a chance to settle in, my dad called and told my mom to start packing. He had only been at Moses Lake for a week when he received orders to report to Casper Air Base in Casper, Wyoming. She recalled what happened next: "I followed as soon as I could get tickets. What a trip! Our berth was an upper one and I put Bobby on the inside and we slept as best we could. In Casper, Bob had found us a basement apartment at 805 E. Third Street."

In 1942, Casper was a town that had not yet recovered from the Great Depression. It had been 13 years since the devastating economic crash on Wall Street, which had caused numerous local banks to shut their doors. In the early thirties, Wyoming's much-relied-upon oil industry had bottomed out, with the agricultural sector following suit shortly thereafter. The outlook for the tiny town was bleak. World War II would end up being its savior.[13] It had been four months since the Japanese attack on Pearl Harbor and the United States declarations of war against the Axis Powers. In that relatively short period, the war machine had been cranked up to full capacity throughout the country. New military installations were popping up everywhere. The government was looking to build an Army air base in the wide-open prairie lands of Wyoming for heavy bomber replacement training; the economically starved town of Casper was chosen for the site.

In March of 1942, construction began on four asphalt runways, each approximately 8,500 feet long.[14] Barracks, hangars, a control tower, and numerous other buildings were all built and operable in less than six months' time. In September, the Casper Army Air Base was awaiting its first pilots for training. John Goss, director of the Wyoming Veterans Memorial Museum, which now stands where the air base once was, describes the transformation of the sleepy town: "The base brought an influx of people into Casper. It employed 2,000 to 2,500 Army Air Forces personnel at any one time, between 500 to 800 civilians and, at its height, served as training ground for some 3,000 pilots, navigators, bombardiers and other crewmen. Therefore, on any given day from 1942 to 1945, there were over 6,000 people on the base. By the war's end, Casper Army Air Base had produced between 16,000 and 20,000 crewmen for combat duty."[15]

My father arrived at Casper Army Air Base for heavy bomber flight training in July of 1943, nine months after it had started operations. Originally, the base had been training pilots on B-17s, but by the time my dad got there, all heavy bomber flying was on B-24s.[16] Hundreds of pilots, co-pilots, and their crews, who were the initial airmen to report to the base, were already flying combat missions in Europe and the Pacific theater as replacement crews. My father was excited about the prospect of flying the B-24 Liberators, and also about meeting the crew he would go into combat with—men he would have to trust with his life. Within days, he met Pat Logan, George Britton, and Joe Spontak, pilot, bombardier, and navigator respectively. Of the four, my dad was the only one married and at 24 years of age, he was the oldest crew member. Logan was 22, Britton and Spontak only 19. Spontak told me decades later that after they flew together for a while and became better acquainted, the members of their bomber crew jokingly referred to my father as "the old man."

Within a week, my mother and brother had settled into the small basement apartment my father had found in town. In California and Texas, all pilots were required to live in barracks, but in Casper, some were allowed to live off base. It was my parents' first place of their own since Bobby's birth. Since the schedules of day or night flight training were posted regularly, my father knew in advance when he could spend precious time with his family. My mother recalled sitting in her apartment playing with my brother, listening to the drone of heavy bombers as they flew overhead during training, knowing her husband and his crew were among them. She smiled, recalling that sometimes and without warning, the engine roar of the B-24s would grow deafening and her little apartment and everything in it would shake violently. Her explanation made me laugh. Although it was illegal and frowned upon by the USAAF, my father would, as he approached the air base for landing, occasionally fly his plane directly over their apartment in a maneuver known as "buzzing." Eventually, Air Command got wind of it, he was reprimanded, and it never happened again.

Every time my father left for the base, my mother would say a little prayer for his safe return. Rumors of B-24 bomber crashes stateside during training were becoming more and more widespread; sadly, they were not rumors at all. There was a multitude of contributing factors, mechanical failure ranking among the highest. By 1943, every USAAF base in the country was under intense pressure to train their pilots and crews for combat duty as quickly as possible. The Army Air Force was suffering staggering casualties overseas, in human lives as well as aircraft losses; the need for replacement

crews was urgent. Therefore, the bombers used for training were up
in the air almost every hour of the day and night. Maintenance crews
were forced to take shortcuts when inspecting the planes. Perhaps a
loose bolt or a damaged flap would go undetected and as a result, ten
men could die in a fiery crash. Due to their lack of experience, pilots
and navigators, most in their early twenties or younger, were sus-
ceptible to making poor decisions in simulated combat situations.
The B-24 Liberator had the reputation of being incredibly difficult to
fly; night landings during training were treacherous and sometimes
deadly. Between 1942 and 1945 at Casper Army Air Base alone, there
were 72 heavy bomber crashes resulting in 135 fatalities.[17] My mother's prayers for my father's safety were certainly warranted.

By August, 1943, my dad had accumulated close to 50 hours
of B-24 flight time at Casper. On September 3, he was ordered

grounded. He had been experiencing breathing problems, especially at higher altitudes. Upon examination by the Casper Army Air Base medical staff, he was diagnosed with a deflected septum, a condition which mandated surgery before he would be allowed to resume flight training. He was operated on shortly thereafter and hospitalized for a few days. Recovery was slow and painful, and he remained grounded until the end of December, a period of almost four months. While the rest of his crew's flight training continued, my father was assigned administrative duties on the base, where he served as assistant director of ground training. In January, he was medically cleared and returned to flying status in the co-pilot pool. Casper was experiencing a particularly harsh winter, as evidenced by a couple of photographs I discovered in the green box. My father, mother, and brother are pictured outside of their apartment with

My brother Bobby
with his parents,
Casper, Wyoming,
Winter 1944

heavy coats and hats, and about a foot of snow on the ground. Although many training flights were canceled due to the severity of the weather, some continued through the winter months.

In April, my father was assigned to a regular crew for overseas duty. Gunners, who been trained in their specific skills elsewhere, were introduced to the men who would round out their crew. From that point on, they trained as one unit, developing the close relationships and strong bonds essential in combat. Flight training continued into May and my father rarely missed a day of flying. The demand for fully-qualified combat bomber crews was at its peak by the middle of 1944, and Casper Army Air Base commanders endeavored to quickly ready them for deployment. The days my parents had to spend together were dwindling, and in early May, my dad received orders to report on May 15 to McCook Air Base in Nebraska. Joe Spontak told me that my father, wanting to be with his wife and son, had requested to be assigned to ground duty, but was denied because of the immediate need for replacement crews overseas.

Pat Logan, Jr., son of the pilot of my dad's crew, told me a harrowing story that he learned from his father, and one that my dad almost certainly did not tell my mom. In the early morning hours of May 14, they were returning from a routine nighttime training flight and were preparing to land. At 8,000 feet, Logan called for the landing gear to be down and locked. My father placed the lever in the correct position, noting that when he did so, the green "locked" light went on. Moments later, the engineer made a visual check from his waist gunner position and also verified that the landing gear was down. They made a smooth landing directly in front of the control tower and, almost immediately, both Logan and my father knew something was drastically wrong. Without warning, the bomber pitched downward and veered perilously to the right. Horrified, they realized that the right landing gear had completely collapsed. Sparks flew everywhere as the fuselage of the Liberator scraped the concrete runway, hurtling toward a row of parked bombers. Logan, Jr. quoted his father as to what happened next: "Bob Kurtz and I had to use every muscle in our bodies to steer our ship away from those planes. Another few feet to the right and we would have taken out about ten of them and we would have lost a lot of men." My father's debriefing statement, given only hours after the incident, corroborated Logan's account: "We made a smooth landing in the center of the runway,

rolled about 75 yards perfectly straight and then started drifting noticeably to the right. The pilot hit left rudder and I hit right throttles
but this had no effect since the right main gear collapsed and pulled
us off the runway."[18] When I asked Joe Spontak about it, he vividly
recalled jumping from the smoking bomber, afraid it would split in
two and catch fire. But they were lucky; their B-24 eventually came
to rest in a field, over a half mile from the control tower.

Although there was major wing and fuselage damage to the Liberator, all crewmen aboard escaped unharmed. Known as a "graduation flight," the nighttime training exercise that had almost cost
them their lives was their last at Casper Air Base. They satisfactorily
completed the course of training for combat crews.

Some 30 years later, Pat Logan, Jr.'s father told his son that further investigation into the training accident of May 14 revealed that
the landing gear had been sabotaged by someone on the maintenance crew, probably a German infiltrator. It was classified information at the time, and therefore did not appear on any of the investiga-
tive reports issued by Casper Air Base. However, Pat's father clearly
recalled learning months later that the saboteur was apprehended
shortly thereafter, immediately tried, found guilty, and sentenced
to death—a sentence that was carried out by firing squad the following day.[19] It is unclear whether or not my father and the rest of
his crew were ever informed about the sabotage that had occurred
that night. They were busy saying goodbyes and getting their personal effects together for deployment to Nebraska the next day. The
constant pressure to get bombers overseas and into action left no
time for reflection.

The day both my parents had been dreading was upon them. Not
knowing if he would ever see his wife and son again, my father spent
the precious little time he had left with them at their apartment. He
played with Bobby and didn't leave Peggy's side until the motor pool
arrived to take him back to the base. He knew that within a couple
of hours, he and his crewmen would be flying to McCook Air Base
for advanced training. With one last hug from his wife and son, he
was on his way.

My mother spent the next few days cleaning the apartment and
packing for her trip back home. She had purposely left one item un-
packed until the last moment, and she smiled wistfully as she put
it in her bag. The night before my dad left, my parents had agreed

on a plan. Not knowing when or if they would see each other again, they decided to divide a pair of their son's slippers, one going to war and one staying home. They became talismans of good luck, with the idea that when my father returned from war, the slippers would be reunited, as would they. It was a decision that would save my father's life.

McCook Air Base, located in southwestern Nebraska, was one of eleven USAAF bases constructed there during the early forties. The War Department selected Nebraska for heavy bomber training sites because much of the state was sparsely populated. Its wide-open flatlands were ideal for bombing and gunnery exercises. In addition, unlike Army airfields on the eastern and western coasts, which were constantly on alert for German or Japanese attacks, McCook was relatively protected.[20] My father's flight logs indicate that his newly assembled crew flew more than 60 hours of simulated combat training at McCook in the month of May alone; day by day, they were becoming more acclimated to working as a unit. With so much time spent together in such close proximity, they began to feel like family.

My father's heavy bomber training runs at McCook were mostly uneventful, with two exceptions that I learned about in conversations with Joe Spontak and Pat Logan Jr., 70 years after they occurred. Spontak recalled an incredibly difficult landing during a fierce sandstorm. Visibility was near zero and as they hit the runway, sand clogged the engines of their B-24, knocking out power. Somehow, they successfully landed without further damage or problems, but Joe said it was one of the most frightening moments of his life.

Pat Logan's father told him another hair-raising story about a forced landing the crew had to make during one of their flights. He remembered doing a routine check of cockpit gauges with my father while flight training somewhere over southwestern Nebraska. Suddenly they froze with fear as they realized that the fuel levels were perilously low. Whether it had been a leak or one of the crewmen's oversights during pre-flight check, no one could be sure. What they *were* sure of was that there was not enough fuel to make it back to McCook. The Nebraska landscape proved to be their saving grace as Logan and my father had no choice but to land in a cornfield. Miraculously, no one was injured and the bomber was only slightly damaged. The same could not be said for their egos after radioing in their position to McCook Air Command.

The sabotaged landing gear at Casper, along with these two incidents and God knows how many more that involved my father, have made me realize that in many ways, I am lucky to be alive. My dad looked death straight in the eye at least three times before even entering combat, and lived to tell about it. Thousands of USAAF airmen training in the States were not so lucky. Chilling stateside statistics show that in the Army Air Force alone, there were 52,651 stateside aircraft accidents over the course of the war, killing 14,903 personnel. Monthly death tallies exceeding 500 were common. In August, 1943, the peak of my father's flight training, 590 airmen died stateside, an average of 19 per day.[21] These were reports of fatalities only; the number of injured airmen must have been much higher.

Civilians like my mother were mostly unaware of these mind-boggling statistics, as the War Department purposely issued only sporadic news of heavy bomber training accidents with fatalities. They say ignorance is bliss; such was the case with my mom. After my father had flown to McCook, she and my brother took a train back east. She stopped in Ohio to see her sister and aunt, hoping that family visits would keep her mind off the dangers my dad faced. Every minute that went by, she missed him a little more, and visions of her husband involved in deadly combat kept her awake at night. Writing letters to him helped a little, but the thought that she might never see him again scared her. She told me once that there were two things that kept her from losing her mind. My father's letters were one, but what really saved her was having my brother to take care of. She said the inner strength she drew from having him with her at all times enabled her to deal with things that were out of her control.

On May 28, 1944, my father and his crew were transferred to Topeka Air Base in Kansas, their last stop before shipping out. According to his flight logs, the crew flew only four hours during the few days he was stationed there. From his initial flight training in Ontario, California, in December of 1943, up to his days in Topeka, he had accumulated a little more than 400 hours of flying. Training had concluded and his crew anxiously awaited their orders, all of them on edge, aware that their deployment to the European Theatre of Operations was imminent. Finally the word came...they would leave the next day, June 8.

My mother had been back in White Plains for only a few weeks when she received the call she had been dreading. Her husband phoned her as soon as he learned his deployment date. They were able to talk for only a few minutes, because other airmen were waiting in lines to call their loved ones, too. There was so much to say; they kept to the essentials. There weren't enough words to say how much they loved each other, but they tried. My father told my mother to be sure to give their son a huge hug and a kiss; my mom told him to be sure to bring back Bobby's slipper, and then they hung up.

My mother and brother would stay in her parents' home, awaiting his return. My father was off to war.

EHRWALD 2001

A S OUR PLANE TOOK OFF, I LOOKED OVER AT MY SON MIKE.
A feeling of warmth and love enveloped me. It was crucial
that I share this journey with him; he wanted to know more
about his grandfather and I could think of no better way for him
to accomplish that than to accompany me. At 20 years old, Mike
displayed a maturity beyond his years. I knew how emotional the
next few days would be and was grateful that he would be right by
my side.

It was August 1, 2001, and we were on our way to a tiny village
called Ehrwald, in the Austrian Alps. I hoped my trip would answer
the myriad questions about my father that had plagued me after
discovering the green box in my attic as an eight-year-old child.
There had been a huge gap of time from that moment to the one that
found me on my way to Europe, but I had never lost my interest,
just my motivation. High school, college, marriage, and family had
consumed my time for the next few decades and, understandably,
the green box and its contents had been put on the back burner. In
the year 2000, a sequence of events changed all that.

My brother Bill had always been interested in our dad's wartime
experiences but, like me, had little information to work with; my
father had said next to nothing about his military life to anyone, including my mother. Not to be denied, Bill decided he would attempt
to locate surviving members of our father's original bomber crew.
His intense search was rewarded with responses from Joe Spontak,
George Britton, and Lee Englehorn, navigator, bombardier, and
gunner respectively. He shared their e-mail messages with me and
the long-neglected spark was rekindled. Now, I not only wanted to
know more about my father, I *needed* to know more. Shortly thereafter, Bill forwarded an e-mail to me from a woman named Debbie
Beson, whose father had been a replacement gunner on my dad's
bomber. She explained that she had just returned from Austria,
where she had climbed a mountain and explored our fathers' crash

site. There were plans to return the following year for a local commemoration of the air battle in the town of Ehrwald. I asked Bill if he was going to make the trip, but his business schedule made it impossible. He sent me a copy of the invitation he had received from a local resident, Gerd Leitner, in case I might be interested in attending. I opened it and read the first paragraph, and my mind was made up. This wasn't only rekindling the spark, it was throwing gasoline on the fire! The opportunity to learn more about the father I never knew had fallen into my hands and I wasn't going to let go of it.

Leitner's e-mail to my brother was extremely informative. He not only explained what the commemoration would entail, but, more importantly, why he had decided to host the ceremony. The original idea had come from another gentleman, Keith Bullock. An Englishman, Bullock served with a British radar unit stationed in southern Italy from 1944-45, not far from many of the USAAF bases located there. One of those bases was Pantanella, where my father and the 465th Bomb Group were stationed, flying bombing missions into Germany. On August 3, 1944, Bullock's radar screen picked up an intense firefight raging over the Austrian Alps. He never forgot it.

After the war, he moved close to Ehrwald, Austria, where the battle of August 3 had occurred. As a hobby, he researched the events of that day, which still echoed in his mind. He devised a plan to honor the 80 airmen of the 465th Bomb Group that had flown that day by erecting small monuments at the locations of all eight B-24 crash sites. His plan was to have bronze plaques mounted on crosses, every one of them bearing the names of the ten crewmen on board each bomber, citing whether they had been killed in action or taken prisoner of war. In 1998, Bullock met Leitner and they became fast friends when Gerd told Keith he had witnessed the battle firsthand as a child. The two of them spent countless hours researching the battle on the Internet and conducting interviews with local villagers. Through hard work and perseverance, they obtained the names of all 80 American airmen and eight German fighter pilots shot down during aerial combat that day. With that information in hand, Bullock and Leitner decided not only to erect memorials at the crash sites, but also to invite survivors of the air battle or their next of kin to a ceremony in Ehrwald on August 3, 2001, to commemorate the battle that had changed so many peoples' lives in so many ways 57 years earlier. Sadly, three months before the ceremony, Keith

Bullock suffered a crippling stroke and was unable to attend. Leitner was left to manage the final preparations for our visit. But I will be forever thankful to both of them for planning the life-changing event that found my son and me on our way to Europe in August of 2001.

Our flight to Munich consisted of non-stop dialogue between Mike and me. There were so many questions we hoped to have answered by the end of our trip and we spent most of our time compiling a list of them so as not to forget a single one. Before we knew it, we had arrived, and after a minimal delay in customs, we boarded a local train for the short ride to Munich. Approaching the city, we had a wonderful view of its skyline, which features both modern and centuries-old architecture. I wondered how many of the newer buildings had been built to replace structures destroyed by British and American carpet bombings during World War II. Had my father piloted one of those bombers? If so, there is no doubt in my mind that the huge loss of innocent lives caused by those aerial raids would have haunted him for the rest of his life.

After checking into our hotel, we enjoyed a nice German meal, and retired for the night. Unfortunately, upon awakening the next morning, I found that the nice German meal had transformed into a horrendous case of food poisoning. I had planned this trip so carefully; I had traveled to Europe for the adventure of a lifetime, but I hadn't planned for this. Regardless, there was no turning around now.

Our plans were to return to the airport where we would be met by our host, Gerd Leitner. I was anxious to meet him. From the day that Bill had passed on Leitner's invitation, we had e-mailed each other several times and I had learned why Gerd was so enthusiastic about organizing the commemoration of the air battle. As a seven-year-old child, Leitner had been sitting with his mother, Maria, having lunch on his outdoor patio on August 3, 1944. He loved to hike in the Austrian Alps surrounding his village and the day was ideal for his adventure, bright blue skies and not a cloud in sight. His mother smiled at him, knowing he was anxious to finish his lunch and head for the mountains. At that moment, a low rumble was heard coming from the skies to the north of their village and it was getting louder by the second. They immediately recognized the sound; it was one they had heard often over the past few months. It was normal to hear formations of American B-24 bombers returning from their missions in

Germany, creating a thunderous roar as they flew over Ehrwald. That day, however, was different, and they weren't sure why. It was 11:55 a.m. They instinctively looked up into the skies above them and were surprised to see the planes flying more slowly than usual, as if suspended in the sky. Gerd sensed something else out of the ordinary. The usual cacophony of the returning bombers was accompanied by a noise that sounded to him like a swarm of bees. But they weren't bees; they were Messerschmitt 109s and Focke-Wulf 190s, German fighter planes, and they filled the skies around the American planes.

Gerd Leitner, circa 1944
Courtesy Gerd Leitner

Suddenly, the fighters attacked from all sides, opening fire on the helpless bombers. There was return fire from most of the B-24 gunner positions and the sky grew black as both American and German aircraft caught fire, exploded, and came hurtling earthward, spewing smoke in every direction. It was over in less than a minute. In one of his e-mails, Leitner remembered: "My mother told us to hide in the house. We had seen some of the crashes with bigger and smaller fires and a lot of parachutes falling from the sky. The authorities kept us away from all crash sites for the next few days." Witnessing the carnage in the skies over his village had a dramatic effect on Leitner's life. Half a century passed, but he never left Ehrwald. He married, was successful in business, and lived a comfortable, normal life. The only reminder of the air battle he had witnessed as a child was a one-minute cessation of all local activity every year on August 3 at 11:55 a.m., when bells toll and echo throughout the valley.

Gerd was waiting for us at the airport with Debbie Beson and members of her family. After introductions, we talked excitedly about the upcoming events and Leitner's enthusiasm was contagious. I liked him immediately. When I had heard that he would be our guide for the climb to my father's crash site, I had wondered how a man almost 65 years old could possibly hike over 6,000 feet up into the Austrian Alps. Now I knew. He was an extremely fit individual, a vegetarian, and a non-drinker who hiked regularly. He had light brown hair, hardly a wrinkle on his face, and could easily have passed for someone 20 years younger. My concerns about Leitner had been premature; he obviously was not going to have any problem climbing to the crash site.

The drive from the airport to Ehrwald was one I won't easily forget. I had rented a car and our plans were to follow Gerd, who was driving Debbie and her family. I hadn't realized that the largest portion of the trip called for us to drive on the Autobahn. I had heard and read stories about the high-speed German expressway, but nothing prepared me for what happened next. Within seconds of entering the Autobahn, the rear of Leitner's car became a small dot in front of me. Not knowing where we were going, I had no choice but to try to catch up to him. I jammed the accelerator to the floor and off we went! I looked at the speedometer and realized it registered in kilometers, so I had no idea how fast we were traveling. I eventually caught up to Leitner and when we got off the expressway, he pulled into a nearby parking lot. He got out of the car with a huge grin on his face, especially when seeing how white with fear my face was. He asked if I knew the speed we had been driving and I couldn't even venture a guess, although I knew it was by far the fastest I had ever driven. When he finally stopped laughing, he told me. We had been driving a little over 130 miles an hour!

We got back in our cars and it wasn't too long before we had crossed the border into Austria. I had come down from the natural high I experienced as we sped down the Autobahn. Now, I was on more of a spiritual high, one of quiet reverence, knowing that part of my father's life and his wartime experiences had occurred in this part of the world. I sensed that in some way, he was right there with me, putting his arm around me and saying, "C'mon, son, let me show you where it all happened and what it was like." My silent response: "Okay, Dad, I'm with you every step of the way."

The last hour of our trip evoked every emotion imaginable. We passed through the town of Garmisch, Germany, and while the name sounded vaguely familiar, I couldn't pinpoint why. Leitner later told me, "That's where your father was transported after being taken prisoner in Ehrwald." Incredible. I had driven by the building where my dad once stood dazed and bleeding. I tried to imagine the fear and mindset of the American airmen as they anticipated their initial interrogation. I wondered if the Germans had beaten my father.

As we continued on to Ehrwald, I was entranced by the tranquility and serenity all around. A meandering brook paralleled the road. It was a warm August day and I rolled down the window. We stopped at an intersection and I could hear the trickling stream; it was a soothing sound. Blue-green waters sparkled in the late summer sun. The irony of the moment was not lost on me. This idyllic country road that traversed the lower Austrian Alps could not have been more perfect in August of 2001. Decades earlier, captured prisoners had been marched to Garmisch over the same route. Pink flower petals lay on the road's surface where 57 years before, spattered drops of crimson blood had fallen.

We were approaching the village and I began to make a few mental notes of the men and women I was scheduled to meet. I decided to categorize them in terms of importance to me, a personal triage system. Whoever could provide the most information about my father would be on top of the list. Men like Gerd Leitner and Joe Spontak took priority. I was excited about talking to Hilde Richter, who, I was told, had a very special reason for wanting to meet me. Why had a 65-year-old Austrian woman, herself an Ehrwald native, asked Leitner to arrange a meeting specifically with me? I had been informed that two German fighter pilots involved in the air battle of August 3, 1944, would also be in attendance and I was anxious to hear what they had to say. Last, but certainly not least, I wanted to spend some time with Debbie Beson, the daughter of Tony Jezowski, the top turret gunner on my father's Liberator. She said she had a very interesting story to tell me about the air battle that would make me proud and enable me to gain more insight into the man my dad was. All these people to meet in only three days. I promised myself to make every minute count, hoping that I could learn as much as possible about my dad and make friendships that would last the rest of my life.

We pulled up to the Hotel Tirolerhof, our place of lodging and the center of activities for the next couple of days. Gerd pointed upward to a valley that lay between two large mountains. "Jim, that valley is known as the Ehrwalder Alm. It is where your father was captured by German soldiers. Another 2,000 meters higher is the Brendlkar, the area of the mountain where his Liberator crashed. There are still many parts of the plane at the site. I will take you and your son up there two days from now and we will explore the wreckage. If all goes well, I believe we can find a souvenir plane part that has something to do with your father and you can take it home with you."

I could barely breathe. I couldn't imagine what Leitner had seen in previous hikes to the crash site that would be recognizable as something pertaining to my dad. I knew that his bomber had burned for two days after crashing into the mountain. I looked at Gerd; he smiled, knowing that his surprise would blow me away.

I needed to slow my heart beat. I stood back and took a couple of minutes to admire my surroundings. It was impossible to imagine being in a more beautiful place. Snow-capped, slate-grey mountains towered over Ehrwald. The meadows and valleys were the plushest I had ever seen. Their emerald-green hue reminded me of Irish post-cards. Although caught up in the moment, my mind wandered back to the past. Fifty-seven years earlier, Leitner had witnessed a scene of hell and destruction that left a permanent mark on his beloved village. I now understood his obsession to commemorate that day.

Mike and I entered the hotel and Gerd introduced us to the owner, his brother, Jorg. He had been only three years old at the time of the air battle, so with no recollection of the event, he was spared the memories that his brother and fellow Ehrwaldians lived with. Jorg was a gracious man and proudly showed off his beautiful hotel, explaining that Joe Spontak, Pat Logan Jr., and numerous other participants in the commemoration would also be staying there.

As if on cue, a tall, pleasant-looking gentleman in his seventies approached our group. By now everyone had been handed name tags and as he drew nearer, his name came into focus. I couldn't believe my eyes. It was Joe Spontak, my father's navigator on the Liberator's crew. He looked at my name tag and said, "Why, I'll be damned! So you're Jim Kurtz. I trained and flew with your father." He extended his hand to shake mine and I held his vise-like grip, not wanting to let go. How many times had my dad shaken this man's hand during their war years together? Once again, an overwhelming calm engulfed me, as it would countless times in the next few days. I could feel my father's presence; he was standing there with me and I embraced his company.

My questions for Spontak were endless. My mother had always told me how wonderful and loving my father was and what a great family man and husband he had been. Here was a person who knew my dad in an entirely different context, as a man he had to trust with his life, someone with whom he had shared the horrors of war. They knew each other inside out; they had to in order to survive. Hundreds of hours were spent training together, as well, I'm sure, as a few hours enjoying a beer or two. I told Joe that I had brought along a tape recorder and asked him if he wouldn't mind recounting the time he had spent with my dad during their wartime service. He was happy to oblige. It required a quiet area with no interruptions, so I suggested we meet at a table later, when the dining room would be closed.

It was almost dinnertime and Jorg had spared no expense providing a delightful buffet with numerous mouth-watering dishes with a local flavor. Still feeling the effects of my meal in Munich, it was all wasted on me. Leitner assured me that if I wasn't feeling better by the next morning, he would contact the local doctor.

I entered the dining room to join the festivities. There were still numerous people I needed to talk to before the commemoration the following day. The atmosphere in the reception room was electric. Gerd waved me over to an area where he was talking with my son and an older woman. "Jim, I'd like you to meet Hilde Richter. She was also a young child living here during the war. She has something she wishes to share with you about your father." We sat down to hear what she had to say, our curiosity piqued. Richter handed out copies of her story for our reference. We read it and sat there stunned. Hilde and her mother and brother were on a picnic the morning of August 3, 1944, in Ehrwald. She witnessed the air battle, saw my father captured and beaten, but not killed, and explained the reason he was spared. This is her story:

> It was in August in 1944 when it all happened. On the third of August my mother, a German woman, my little brother and myself went to the Ehrwalder Alm nearby our village. In the morning of this special day we set off to go there. It was a beautiful day. The Second World War was still going on. But life in a little village like Ehrwald was still safe. We children didn't

realize the tragedy of the war. But suddenly the war was very close to us too. In the air was a fight between American bombers and German fighters going on. We had no chance at all to look for a proper shelter. So we stood under a little pine tree and watched the airplanes and parachutes coming down. After a few minutes the fight was over. When we reached the Ehrwalder Alm to have lunch there we met the first American pilot who had landed with his parachute near the lake Seebensee. I felt sorry for him; he had baby shoes in his bag.[1]

I tried to comprehend what I had just heard and read. The odds of meeting a total stranger thousands of miles from home who had seen my father 57 years earlier were minuscule. Hilde was a delightful woman and extremely proud that her story would be a part of the commemoration. We separated ourselves from the rest of the group and Mike videoed a more thorough account of her memories of a family picnic on the Ehrwalder Alm. Much to my delight and amazement, every detail of that day was still very clear in her mind despite the passage of time.

Still reeling from hearing Richter's story, I found myself sitting in a bit of a daze. I came out of it as I heard my name called. Once again, it was Leitner motioning for Mike and me to join him and a couple of elderly gentlemen at their table in the dining room. "Jim, I would like you to meet Willi Unger and Oskar Bösch. They were German fighter pilots in the battle over Ehrwald." Unger was the first pilot I shook hands with and as I looked into his eyes, they seemed filled with sadness. We couldn't communicate in words; he spoke only German. We connected in a different way: the horrors of war had affected both of us throughout our lives. He lost friends and comrades at a dizzying pace throughout the war. Although my father was to die seven years after the war's end, in my mind there was never any doubt that it was the war that eventually killed him. For the next two days, I never saw Willi Unger smile. Numerous photographs taken during the commemoration bear this out. His face was always solemn. He had done his job admirably while in the service and had probably spent years trying to erase painful war memories. Although the festivities must have made those memories resurface, he was a total gentleman throughout and it was an honor for me to have met him.

Oskar Bösch was just the opposite. He smiled constantly and relished in telling his account of the air battle. Unlike others I had met at the commemoration, Bösch came across as a man who would still have enjoyed fighting in a war. He had high praise for Adolph Hitler and was adamant about letting people know it. Bösch approached me and read my name tag. It took him a few seconds to put two and two together but once he did, a huge smile broke out on his face. "Ah, Herr Kurtz, did you know that I am the fighter pilot that shot your father's B-24 down? It was a beautiful morning and our fighters came out of a low cloud cover. We were flying Messerschmitt-109s and Focke-Wulf 190s. We had four fighters for every one bomber in your dad's formation. It was over very quickly because they had no chance. Ja, it was like shooting ducks in a pond!"

I didn't know what to say. I didn't hate the man for shooting down my father's plane; he was only doing his job. However, it galled me that he was so damned happy about it. As he recounted the air battle, his eyes flickered with excitement, and I quickly tired of our conversation. It didn't seem to faze him that he was bragging about his exploits as a fighter pilot on August 3, 1944, to the son of a man he almost killed that day. Mike, seeing that I was uncomfortable, suggested we head upstairs. Before leaving, I sought out Joe Spontak to reschedule our tape session. The meetings with Richter and Bösch had exhausted me, so I went off for some badly needed sleep.

Gerd called the doctor the next morning and Dr. Poll picked me up at the hotel himself and drove me to his office, where he immediately hydrated me with intravenous fluids. As I lay there, we had a wonderful conversation. I explained that I would be climbing to my dad's crash site the next day, one way or the other, knowing that a 2,000-meter ascent is difficult even for a totally healthy person. It turned out that Dr. Poll was an avid hiker. He was well aware of the unveiling ceremony that afternoon in Ehrwald and was also a bit of a World War II buff. He promised to do everything medically possible to enable me to make the climb. A few hours later, he took me back to the hotel and wished me luck for the following day's activities.

As he drove off, I looked up at the sky and surrounding countryside. The realization of what day it was overwhelmed me and I had to sit down on the front stairs of the hotel. It was August 3, 2001.

Fifty-seven years before, at exactly this time of day, above this peaceful village, all hell had broken loose.

At 3:00 p.m., the quiet little jewel in the Austrian Alps known as Ehrwald was quiet no longer. The village was a whirlwind of preparations for the unveiling of the monument in the center of town. Television and radio stations from all over Austria and Germany came to cover the event. Many Europeans and Americans had traveled great distances to attend. A misty rain began to fall but it couldn't dampen the spirits of the celebrants. Leitner's and Bullock's perseverance was about to be rewarded. The intent of the ceremony was not only to honor the men who had died in the air battle but also to embrace new friendships that would grow from one common denominator: a desire to bring together men who at one point in time had tried to kill each other, to let them get to know one another and, hopefully, to forgive and forget the terrors of war.

The event started with a parade through town led by an Austrian marching band; survivors of the air battle or their family members were next in line. I beamed with pride as I strode up the street alongside Debbie Beson, Joe Spontak, and others. We were met at the center of town by hundreds of excited people who had filled the square to enjoy all the pomp and circumstance. The mayor of Ehrwald gave a speech welcoming the throng, which was followed by the unveiling of the monument by Debbie Beson. Her daughter, Connie, read the names of each American airman killed in action on August 3, 1944. There were 30 names in all and it was a sobering moment as she crisply delivered each name and rank, her voice resonating in the hushed silence. A military chaplain then blessed the monument and the local rifle club fired a salvo that boomed throughout the valley. Next was a speech given by Colonel Bruce Boevers, the highest ranking American officer in the region. Finally, the local musicians played an Austrian tune called "Comrades," and looking around, I noticed many eyes filling up with tears. I could see Joe Spontak flanked by Willi Unger and Oskar Bösch and the three of them had their arms around each other. Unger raised his hand in a humble salute as the last few chords of "Comrades" could be heard echoing off the mountainsides.

We gathered back at the hotel for the dinner buffet and everyone was still exhilarated from the ceremony. Most of the participants would be leaving the next day. Old enemies had become new friends.

Family members of the men involved in the air battle, especially those KIA (Killed in Action), finally had some closure. Scores of questions about August 3, 1944 had been answered. Everyone agreed it had been a rewarding day.

My thoughts turned to the next day's climb. Physically, I felt stronger and more confident that I would make it up the mountain. I started to go upstairs when I remembered my meeting with Joe Spontak was in five minutes. In the excitement of the day's festivities, I had almost forgotten what I had considered to be the most important event of my trip. My wish to sit down with a man who knew my father well was about to become a reality. I grabbed my tape recorder and headed for the dining room.

Joe was waiting for me. I ordered schnapps for the two of us and turned on my tape recorder, and we spent the next hour talking about my dad. I was like a little schoolboy constantly raising my hand to interrupt him with "just one more" question. I hung on his every word as he described training with my father, first in Casper, then McCook, and finally, Topeka. Joe's stories, such as the one about when they were forced into an emergency landing in a Nebraska cornfield, captivated me. My research into training accidents involving B-24s was extensive, but this was the first time I had heard that my father had come close to becoming one of those statistics and it stunned me. Spontak recounted endless hours of flight training with my father. He remembered practicing landings both day and night, some more dangerous than others due to extreme weather conditions. He recalled that he was often grounded at the air base in Casper during the winter of 1943–1944 due to snow and sub-freezing temperatures. Joe said he had met my mother and brother, who were living near the base in Casper, and remembered her as a very beautiful woman. He also told me about the intense heat while training in the Midwest and recalled a particularly bad dust storm in Kansas that caused their B-24 engines to stall out during a training exercise.

Finally, Spontak described how their crew had assembled in Topeka, to pick up their aircraft in preparation for the flight overseas. They flew to Manchester, New Hampshire, where they remained for two days before setting off for Gander, Newfoundland—their last stop in North America before flying to Europe. He explained that although the original flight plan called for crossing the northern Atlantic and then continuing on through England and France to their final destination in Italy, those plans were scrapped at the last moment. It was early June of 1944 and the Allied invasion of Normandy was underway. This forced my father and his crew to fly south through the Azores. Joe said they had to be very careful to land on the right island in the Azores because many of them were controlled by Germany. Next was a stop in Marrakesh, Morocco, and finally on to Tunis, where they picked up the bomber in which they would fly all of their combat missions. She was a B-24H Liberator and they christened her *Sugar Baby*. The team complete, their final destination was Pantanella Air Base in Italy, where the 465th Bomb Group began operations in the early summer of 1944.

The highlight of my conversation with Spontak was a story he told of their flight across the Atlantic. Pat Logan and my father had been taking turns at the controls of the B-24 and had flown over the ocean for quite a few hours. Joe, who was navigating, called up to the cockpit on the radio, concerned about their location. He laughed as he recalled, "I got on the radio and said 'Pat, Bob, come in, over.' No answer. I tried a second and third time, still no answer. Finally, I left my position to find out what the hell was going on. I'll be damned if both Pat and your dad weren't sound asleep. I shook them awake and returned to my station immediately. I had been right to be concerned about our location. We had drifted hundreds of miles off our course. I had to use the stars for navigation to get back on course because we were over water. I never let them forget that night."

For the latter part of our conversation, we talked about the harrowing events of the air battle. Joe related the details of his bailing out, capture, interrogation, and eventual imprisonment at Stalag Luft III, which was the same POW camp as my father's. He visited my dad at his barracks periodically and felt it important to stress that my father was in a depressed state. I'm sure there were degrees of depression for all the prisoners, but for those who were married and had children, it was understandably more acute. His stories of imprisonment, camp conditions, and the infamous "Forced March" contributed to my understanding of what my father went through. After the prisoners' evacuation from Stalag Luft III in late January of 1945, Spontak never saw my father again.

I thanked Joe for giving me an insight into the man my father was. I excused myself and headed upstairs. I thought about the climb and my excitement grew, knowing I was finally going to see my father's crash site. As I laid my head down on my pillow, the last thought before I dozed off was, "What could Gerd Leitner's surprise possibly be?"

After a night of tossing and turning, I was awakened by my son who had been out on the town until some ungodly hour the night before; somehow he looked incredibly fresh. I had been anticipating this day for months. It seemed rather dark in our room but I dismissed that thought by reasoning that it was still early morning. I walked across the room to the window, anxious to find out what type of weather we would have for the climb. I lifted the shade, looked out, and couldn't believe what I was looking at. Our room had been dark because the entire valley and the mountains that surrounded our hotel were shrouded in black, menacing clouds. The sideways rain and torrential downpour reminded me of the nor'easters back home. I cursed under my breath as I wondered how the weather was going to affect our climb to the Brendlkar. I began to panic, knowing that this was the only day we could hike to the crash site; our plane reservations for the next day could not be canceled. I worried about my physical condition, my age, the wet footing for our ascent, and every other possible thing, with the end result being one massive knot in my stomach.

Gathering my resolve, I got dressed and went downstairs into the hotel foyer to meet with our group. I stepped outside and was greeted by a cold, harsh wind. The temperature was in the forties with a wind chill factor in the thirties. Our first priority was to go to Leitner's sports shop in the village where Gerd outfitted us with new rain jackets and climbing poles. He explained that while the present weather in Ehrwald left a lot to be desired, it could be entirely different another 2,000 meters up at the Brendlkar. Mike took this to heart and decided to wear shorts, arguing, "It's August." I wondered if funding his education at Boston College had been wise after all. To this day, I always smile when looking at pictures of him standing in the snow at the crash site...in his shorts.

We returned to the hotel and I was happy to see that the rain was letting up. Our group of hikers was waiting in the hotel parking lot with huge grins of anticipation; none of us was going to let the weather spoil our adventure. Greeting us were Debbie Beson, her husband Tim, and daughter, Connie. I gave Debbie a hug of appreciation, thanking her for encouraging me to make the trip to Ehrwald. Colonel

Jim with his son Mike, halfway up to the Brendlkar crash site, August 4, 2001

Boevers and his wife were there, along with a few people from town. Rounding out our group was our guide, Gerd Leitner, and Joe Spontak. At 76 years old, Joe was unlikely to complete the grueling climb.

We piled into cars that took us to the base of the mountain, thus reducing our climb by a few hundred meters and close to an hour in time. We parked in a lot next to a beautiful valley filled with cows and sheep. Gerd said it was called the Ehrwalder Alm and I instinctively grabbed Mike's arm in a white-knuckle grip. We were standing in the valley where Hilde Richter had watched the Germans capture my father. Once again, I felt my father's presence and while it comforted me, it also saddened me to think that his memory of this valley and the events that occurred here must have always laid heavy on his mind.

We began our ascent in a light drizzle. After about 200 meters, Spontak decided to head back to the village. Our group of twelve now began the climb in earnest. It was steep at points, so we crisscrossed through the sparse brush. Once we had trekked over 1,000 meters, it became more difficult as the mountainside became a steeper slope of small pieces of shale and rock. The dampened scree made it hard to secure a foothold. Adrenaline kicking in was a huge help. I jokingly pestered Gerd to disclose his big secret but he would have none of it. While maddening, it was actually helpful; there's nothing like curiosity to distract from aching legs and lungs.

I looked down into the valley and realized that we were over 2,000 meters above sea level. Leitner turned around to address our group. "The crash site of the B-24 Liberator *Sugar Baby* is right over the next hill. Congratulations, you have all succeeded in making the climb to the Brendlkar." Although physically spent, I was on such an emotional high that I wanted to sprint over that last hill. We reached the crest where I stood mesmerized as we looked down into a small glen. Torn pieces of metal lay strewn about, some of them fused to rocks and boulders, a testament to the intense heat generated as *Sugar Baby* burned for two days. What struck me as very odd was the lack of rust on some of the metal parts of the bomber. Leitner provided the explanation. The area where we stood is covered by snow or water for ten and a half months of the year, which surprisingly protects the plane parts from normal effects of nature that could cause corrosion. The snow and water that cover the wreckage also limit the opportunity for exploration of the site; it is only accessible for about six weeks a year.

As I stood there absorbing the scene, Leitner reached into his backpack and extracted something, walked toward me and said, "This is my surprise for you." It was a schematic of the cockpit of a B-24 Liberator. "There is a difference between the design of the pilot seat and the co-pilot seat," he explained. "I have located where both are in the crash site. Using the schematic, we will determine which seat was your father's, remove a piece of it from the wreckage, and you can take it back home with you."

I had already grown very fond of Leitner, but the fact that he had taken the time to research the B-24 so extensively was deeply touching. To ensure that we wouldn't be trying to read an ink-stained diagram in the rain, he had taken the precaution to laminate it. Gerd gestured for me to follow him. He had hiked to the crash site numerous times and scrutinized every piece of the wreckage. It was fascinating to have him not only identify the parts but also explain their function in detail.

In a few moments, we reached an area that contained an extraordinary amount of debris from the downed bomber. Leitner looked at

A section of Robert Kurtz's co-pilot seat from the Brendlkar crash site

his cockpit schematic one more time and knelt down. No words were needed. This was what we had been waiting for. I leaned over to help Gerd extract the piece of torn metal from the wreckage. It took us a while because we had no cutting tools and the aluminum remnants of what was once my father's B-24 cockpit had been fused together as *Sugar Baby* burned. We had to use large rocks to break off a piece of the co-pilot seat, a primitive, but ultimately effective process. My son had been filming our efforts and the smile on my face when we extracted the piece told the whole story. I realized that the last person to have made bodily contact with the rusted metal now in my hands was my father. He sat in this seat for all of his bombing missions; on what was to be his last, my dad had engaged in deadly combat, holding on for dear life as 20mm shells ripped through his plane. He had been injured while sitting on what was now the tangled scrap I held; shrapnel that tore through his leg may have come from a piece of it. As I stood there on the Brendlkar, I realized we were above the clouds. It brought thoughts of being close to heaven and therefore, my dad. Holding his co-pilot seat, I extended my arms toward the skies above me and wept.

After that experience, I figured the remainder of our hike would prove somewhat anticlimactic. Leitner had offered to climb even higher with Connie to show her approximately where her grandfather, Tony Jezowski, had landed after bailing out from his burning plane. Although he and my dad had jumped out almost simultaneously, wind currents had altered their landing points considerably. Mike decided to join them to record their adventure and the rest of us were thankful to take a break. They disappeared into the clouds as they continued their ascent. After close to an hour, they returned with video footage that we all enjoyed later that evening at our hotel.

Gerd pointed to an even higher peak and explained that the body of Staff Sgt. Lawrence Hamilton, a replacement gunner on *Sugar Baby*, had been found there two years after the air battle, still wearing his uniform and bomber jacket. I knew he had been killed in action that day, but that was the extent of my knowledge. Debbie knew quite a bit more because Hamilton and her father had trained on the same flight crew of a different B-24. His story is a tragic one. Hamilton had volunteered to fill one of the positions on *Sugar Baby*'s crew due to an automobile accident the previous night that had injured three men of the original crew. It was a decision that cost him his life. Debbie told us that her father, in one of the rare moments he would talk about the war, had told her about Hamilton's fear of jumping out of a plane. He had confided to Jezowski that he wasn't sure he could gather up enough nerve to bail out. Unlike the paratroopers whose training jumps were practiced from 20,000 feet and above, the bomber crews' only training consisted of jumping off a 20-foot platform in a mock exercise. None of the airmen had any idea how they would react in an actual combat situation. They knew that if a jump of any measurable altitude was required, it meant only one thing: their bomber had been damaged beyond repair in aerial combat. It would be their first and last legitimate jump of the war. If they survived, they became members of the Caterpillar Club, a worldwide organization whose membership included thousands of airmen who had executed the jump and lived to tell about it. My father was one of them.

For many, such as Lawrence Hamilton, fear and indecision would prove lethal. When his body was discovered in 1946, there was no parachute in the area. One crewman said that Hamilton had been unable to find a parachute in the burning aircraft. Perhaps, when he jumped as *Sugar Baby* spiraled earthward, he had hoped the deep snow on the mountainside might cushion his blow; it was not meant to be.

As we headed back down the mountain, I realized I was running out of time to talk to Debbie Beson. She had said earlier in the week that she had a story to tell me about her father and mine. So many surreal moments had already occurred; I figured that whatever she had to say would probably pale in comparison with what I had already heard. I was wrong.

Beson told me that her father, Tony Jezowski, refused to talk about his wartime experiences. He blamed the Germans and his time spent in their prisoner of war camps for his lifelong intestinal maladies. However, when he heard that I would be traveling to Ehrwald for the commemoration, he changed his mind and told her a story, with the request that she pass it on to me when we met in Austria. Her first words caught me totally off guard. "I wouldn't be standing here talking to you if it weren't for your dad. He saved my father's life." As she gazed upward, she continued, "Up in these skies fifty-seven years ago." All I could muster was "How?" She explained that his parachute cords had become entangled in *Sugar Baby*'s torn fuselage during the air battle. My father took precious seconds to free him as their bomber hurtled downward. They both bailed out moments before the B-24 exploded in flames. My dad had been a hero and I had never heard a word of this story from my mother or anyone else. He had chosen to tell no one. Like the majority of the men and women who served in World War II, he felt the only heroes were the ones who never came home.

We returned to the village almost seven hours after we had set out. Everyone agreed that it had been the trip of a lifetime. Now it was time to go home and let the experiences of the last three days sink in. For me, it was also time to figure out what would be the next step in the process to discover more about my father and the man he had been.

B-24 Liberator
Image is from Airforce Image Gallery

Sugar Baby's regular crew—Topeka, 1944
Top row, left to right: George Britton, Robert Kurtz, Pat Logan, Joseph Spontak
Bottom row, left to right: Leland Englehorn, Olis Francis,
David Schreves, John Cooper, Jessie Prince, Leonard Bracken
Francis, Schreves, and Prince did not fly on the day of the air battle.

DEADLY SKIES

I T WAS STILL DARK ON THE PANTANELLA ARMY AIR FORCE Base in southern Italy when the operations clerk woke my father in his tent on August 3, 1944. Stars shone brightly in the sky and as he gazed upward, he smiled. The forecast was for clear skies that day, perfect for completing another bombing mission, one more step in the process of going home. He knew that every airman who was lucky enough to survive 35 combat missions was sent back to the States. Flying particularly dangerous missions counted for two, as did volunteering to replace members from other crews. American bomber crews averaged eight to twelve missions before being shot down or disabled.[1]

My father was hours from flying his twentieth combat mission. He was over one-half of the way to being able to head home to his beloved wife, Peggy, and infant son, Bobby, and the opportunity to scratch off one more mission was exhilarating. Yet it was also daunting; the odds did not favor him. In 1943–1944, the chances of surviving a combat tour without being shot down, captured, or killed, was about 25 percent.[2]

As he headed for breakfast, he tried to clear his head of those odds. He knew that negative thoughts could cloud his mind and he needed to concentrate fully on the mission ahead. Returning to his tent after breakfast, he couldn't help but be aware of the brilliant sunrise on the eastern horizon. A religious man, my father acknowledged that God, creator of the universe, was the origin of all things beautiful in nature. He was also well aware that this faith in God was a key factor that allowed him to deal with the death and horror of war. His was not a "foxhole" religion in which men prayed to God to save their lives. While prayers were certainly a daily ritual for him, they consisted of asking for divine assistance to help him through whatever would transpire.

As he walked to the briefing room, he wondered where today's mission would take them. Would it be a particularly difficult target that might count double for missions? If so, chances were strong they would face fierce opposition from German fighters and the terrifying flak that had become all too familiar.

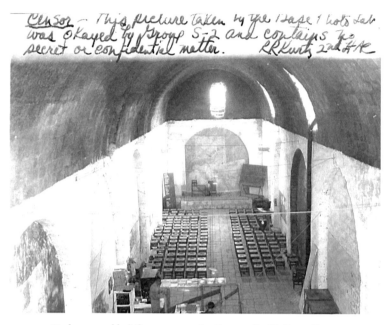

Censor – This picture taken by the 1saqe 1 hots lab was okayed by group S-2 and contains no secret or confidential matter. RRKurth, 2nd H.R.

Underground briefing room on the Pantanella Air Force Base, with my father's note to the censor, 1944

He stepped inside the door of the briefing hall and immediately his eyes were drawn to the huge map on the far wall. My father and the airmen of the thirty-four B-24 Liberators being dispatched that morning were about to learn of their target and its significance. Military intelligence had viable information indicating that a factory in Friedrichshafen, Germany, was producing jet aircraft. In addition, nearby buildings housed the means of producing liquid oxygen, a chemical used in the rocket engines of the dreaded V-2 long-range missiles.[3] The Allied Powers were aware

> "Again you experience a 50-50 feeling. 50 percent happiness because it's going to count double, 50 percent of 'uneasy stomach' because the chances are very good it will be rougher than usual."
> —*Twenty-Four Hours of Flight*

that if production of these jet fighters were allowed to continue, it could adversely alter the course of the war. It had taken years for the Allies to gain air superiority in the European theater and if jets and V-2 missiles became a reality, that superiority could change dramatically. The squadron learned its mission was to bomb the Manzell-Dornier Werke aircraft factory in Friedrichshafen, Germany. Upon learning the target, the crew realized that it was going to be one of their more dangerous missions. The danger was caused by heavy flak, something that struck fear into the airmen's hearts.

The word flak is a shorthand form of the German word *fliegerabwehrkanonen*. In English it means "flyer defense cannons."[4] Flak was radar-directed anti-aircraft fire. There were three types of flak: light, medium, and heavy. Light flak (12.7 or 20mm shells) and medium flak (37mm shells) were shot out of cannons from emplacements on the ground. They were effective primarily for low-flying, slow aircraft. The cannons were easy to dismantle and, because of their relatively light weight, easy to transport. Medium flak was used mainly for defense around German cities. Airmen described the streaming shells as globes of yellow and red, somewhat like tracers. Medium flak shells exploded on contact with the aircraft.[5]

On previous missions, my father and fellow airmen had encountered mostly heavy flak. In 1942, there were more than fifteen thousand 88mm heavy flak cannon emplacements defending Germany. The heaviest cannons wreaked havoc on the bombers; monster 130mm and 150mm shells exploded at heights up to 49,000 feet with deadly accuracy. Unlike the medium flak, which required contact to explode, heavy flak was radar-directed to detonate at pre-set heights, utilizing both altitude-fused and proximity-fused shells.[6]

My father felt the hair rise on his neck as he recalled flying above target sites with heavy flak shells bursting all around him; those deadly black puffs of smoke with searing red bellies haunted him. Heavy flak was a nightmare for bomber crews and its unpredictability presented the biggest challenge. During daylight missions, incoming flak was impossible to detect. It was futile to alter course or swerve to avoid the exploding shells; some aircraft that tried that maneuver ended up flying directly into a different cluster of flak. Over the deafening roar of the four B-24 engines, all that could be heard of the deadly shells was a muffled "krumppf." Split seconds after that dreaded sound, shards of shrapnel could penetrate the aluminum fuselage. They would ricochet wildly throughout the interior, causing massive structural damage, to say nothing of the human carnage. Dad's stomach churned and he had to fight the rise of bile in his throat. Ten Army Air Force crewmen were helplessly cramped and crowded in each Liberator. Highly flammable oxygen canisters and hydraulic fuel lines surrounded them. A flak shell exploding inside an aircraft could turn it into a raging inferno in seconds. It was common to hear stories of airmen's bodies being torn in half from direct flak hits. My father had witnessed B-24s returning to base, their fuselages riddled with shrapnel hits, some large enough for a grown man to crawl through. He trembled as he remembered fellow airmen being transported on stretchers from these shattered planes, limbs torn from their bodies, wounds too gruesome to believe. Some were men with whom he had trained, others complete strangers, but all risking their lives every day.

As the men were briefed about the heavy flak emplacements in and around the Manzell factory, they tried to ignore their fear. They were sitting in a cold underground facility that had been used by local farmers as a hay barn before World War II erupted. Despite the cold, beads of perspiration dotted the foreheads of all the men. Within minutes, the briefing was over. It was not yet 6:00 a.m. In the pastoral-turned-military space, the chaplain rose to offer a prayer to calm the airmen.

"It is a very impressive sight, the men sitting with bowed heads in this old stone building. You feel very close to God."

After the briefing, trucks waiting outside quickly took the crews to their bombers. The airmen began a well-rehearsed procedure, checking out all functions of their B-24s. It was time consuming and tedious, but everyone knew that any malfunction could be catastrophic. Each crew member had a series of checks for his position. The pilot, co-pilot, navigator, and bombardier checks were more detailed and required extra time. Their complex pre-flight procedures included: opening and closing of bomb bay doors, turning the fuel valves on to check the quantity of fuel in the tanks, adjusting pilot and co-pilot seats, switching engines on and off, and priming the turbo chargers, among many others. All ten men were integral to the process.

My father was co-pilot of a B-24 Model H Liberator, plane designation REDF#42-52498, which the crew had christened *Sugar Baby*. They were members of the 15th Air Force, 55th Combat Wing, 780th Bomb Squadron, 465th Bomb Group. As they awaited take-off, he thought back to all the events that had led up to this moment, the years of training in the States, and the hundreds of hours spent with the crew. It was a group of men he had grown to love, and also knew he had to trust with his life. Although substitution was a common occurrence, it concerned him that three regular members of his bomber crew were missing. The night before, they had been in an automobile accident and, due to injuries sustained, were unable to fly. He knew replacements would be well-trained and capable, but he was unable to dismiss the feeling of uneasiness, knowing that one third of the men were new to *Sugar Baby*

He quickly reviewed the crew in his mind. Sitting to his left was the pilot, Lawrence Crane. He had piloted *Sugar Baby* since its arrival in Italy. Pat Logan, who had flown as their pilot throughout hundreds of hours of training in the States, had been mysteriously replaced by Crane when they arrived at Pantanella. Logan was well liked; Lawrence Crane was not. The crew knew him as a brilliant

Co-pilot's position (right side) in the cockpit of a B-24 Liberator
Courtesy National Museum of the U.S. Air Force

pilot but an unpopular one, not unlike a gifted surgeon with an appalling bedside manner. He insisted on being called Lieutenant Crane, never Larry or Lawrence. He consistently volunteered for dangerous missions, leaving many wondering if he had some sort of death wish. He was condescending towards his crew and, at least once, my dad intervened when interactions became heated. George Britton, the regular bombardier on *Sugar Baby*, said, "I have a rec- ollection of your father, at the crew's request, trying to talk sense into Lt. Crane. I also remember a replacement gunner threatening to shoot Crane and me talking him out of his fury." The uneasy feeling my father experienced that morning was not only due to three sub- stitute airmen, but realizing as well that the temperamental Crane would be in the cockpit with him.

My father relaxed a bit knowing that his regular navigator and best friend on the crew, Joe Spontak, was reviewing his charts. His navigational skills were impeccable, which was essential for the success of every mission. In a supine position underneath the nose turret of the plane was the bombardier, George Britton. Dad knew that Britton had the most important job on the flight crew. During the bombing phase of a mission, it was George's job to take control of the aircraft via autopilot. Amidst the chaos, he had to sight in on his target with a Norden bombsight and release tons of bombs with ac- curacy.[7] Over the target area, he had to ignore enemy fighters, heavy flak, and the very real possibility of personal injury. George was bril- liant and my father trusted him more than any other member of the crew, even though he was only 19 years old.

Next, Dad checked on the remaining three members of his orig- inal crew. Lenny Bracken, his engineer, was at his station near the top turret. He was responsible for the technical functions of the B-24 and, as flight mechanic, it was his job was to let the pilots know about engine condition and fuel usage. When the plane was under attack, Bracken operated the top turret gun.

John Cooper's position, radio operator, was toward the center of the plane above the bomb bay doors. He was in charge of all com- munication, not only with other aircraft in their formation, but with Operations Command on the ground. He also occupied one of the waist gunner positions during attack and was trained in first aid. At 33 years old, Cooper was the oldest crew member. Finally, Dad checked on Lee Englehorn, the ball turret gunner and assistant radio man. This position was usually reserved for the smallest of the crewmen. During combat, he was confined to a Plexiglas-encased bubble on the belly of the aircraft. His position was subject to severe temperatures and frequently the ball turret gunner, after hours of flying at altitudes of 30,000 feet, would return to base with various degrees of frostbite.

The three remaining crewmen were an unknown entity. First, he met Charlie Sellars, tail gunner. The tail was one of the most dangerous gunner positions, because most German fighters chose to attack the rear of the bombers. Tail gunners suffered exceptionally high casualties. Next was Lawrence Hamilton, filling in at the nose turret position. While this position allowed for the best vantage point, it was also another favorite target of enemy fighters. With the pilot, co-pilot, navigator, and bombardier within a few feet of the nose gunner, a direct hit from an enemy fighter's deadly cannons could conceivably wipe out half the crew of a B-24. Lastly, Dad shook hands with Tony Jezowski, who manned the top turret gun and also served as assistant engineer. All ten crewmen had secured their positions and prepared for takeoff. The substitute airmen quickly acclimated to *Sugar Baby*. They had volunteered to fly that day, knowing their mission would be counted double.

After the introduction of new crew members, my father focused on his job as co-pilot, knowing he would need all his wits and training just to get the plane off the ground. As they taxied into position, he glanced at his watch. It was 6:44 a.m. and a cloudless sky boded well for sighting the target area later in the day. There was the ever-present fear of prop wash as the bombers began their take-off. A fully fueled and bomb-loaded B-24 weighed close to 30 tons, and it was no easy feat to get it in the air.[8] A collective sigh of relief could be heard from all crew members as they began their ascent.

The next period of flying took them over friendly territory. Their training had physically prepared the men of *Sugar Baby* for the rigors of battle, but the majority of them still had not found a way to cope mentally. Agonizing questions loomed large in each crew member's mind. They were questions they had asked themselves repeatedly on previous sorties and today was no different. Was the sky over their mission's target area going to be swarming with German fighters and deadly flak? Would they be able to bomb the factory effectively? Would they return to base in one piece? Each airman

> "You start to pray, little, short, impromptu prayers that you'll be saying silently for the next three or four hours. They help immeasurably—these prayers—they give you a feeling of calmness and courage not otherwise to be found."

had a different way of dealing with his in-flight down time. Some whistled or sang their favorite songs. Familiar verses from "Chattanooga Choo Choo" or "Boogie Woogie Bugle Boy of Company B" were heard on the men's headphones. While for the most part woefully off key, the music lit up their faces; thoughts invariably turned to home and loved ones back in the States. Some men chose to read books or magazine articles to while away the time; others tried to sleep. My father found peace in prayer.

Sugar Baby flew northward across the Adriatic Sea, one of many B-24 Liberators flying in close formation in "boxes" of six planes each. Some bombers had returned to base due to mechanical failures. *Sugar Baby* was assigned to "Charlie Box."[9] My father often had to fly his plane in tight formation with a full bomb load. The 60,000-pound Liberator was difficult to maneuver; steering was a full-time job, requiring strength and endurance from both pilot and co-pilot. During close formation flying, the massive planes' wingtips were within feet of each other. It was not uncommon to lose a B-24 as a result of one plane's wings clipping the wings of another. During missions, great care was taken to avoid being hit by bombs of one's own squadron. Nevertheless, numerous B-24 crewmen perished from "friendly fire."

> "Kicking thirty odd tons of airplane around in close formation has no parallel that I know of in civilian life. You must be alert literally every second, and the tension thus produced, plus the physical fatigue, evidences itself in the sweat pouring from your body."

As the crew of *Sugar Baby* approached enemy territory, the songs and prayers ceased; everything became strictly business. Gunners test-fired their 50-caliber machine guns and equipped themselves for the cold temperatures of high altitude. Oxygen masks and flak suits were put on.

> "Before long the oxygen mask becomes uncomfortable and the flak suit feels three times its weight as it drags on your shoulders and rubs against the cords in your neck."

As *Sugar Baby* neared the target, all members of the crew were intensely focused on their tasks. Cloud cover was causing a problem, lengthening the time they had to stay over the target. The men in the gun turrets almost forgot the cold and discomfort, hell-bent as they were on keeping enemy fighters at bay. The sound of each man's voice echoed in their headsets as they screamed out positions of fighters that filled the skies.

> "Perhaps the fighters that appear aren't friendly—they're Jerries and coming in. Somehow the formation becomes even tighter, gunners call them off around the clock—"There's two of them high at three o'clock movin' around to four. You've got 'em, Dave." You sit there tensely as you hear the guns chatter, you wait for the answering "smacks" as the enemy tracers find your ship but this time he doesn't get you. Dave got one and scared the other away. You wish you had the power to award medals—he'd get the Congressional Medal and right now!

The pilot and co-pilot listened for communications from other bombers in their formation. *Sugar Baby* shuddered violently as flak bursts exploded all around, but no one could pay too much attention to it...destroying the factory was the job at hand. Finally the clouds below opened. At 11:12 a.m., bombardier George Britton took command of the aircraft and sighted in on the Manzell-Dornier factory. The familiar "bombs away" call resonated through the crewmen's headphones; *Sugar Baby* shook as her bomb load was released over the target. Twenty-eight Liberators dropped a total of 278 bombs on the factory that day.[10]

The 465th Bomb Group had received citations for accumulating a hit ratio over 75 percent. It was the highest rating of any bomb group, not only from Pantanella, but from every other base in Italy as well.[11] They were equally effective on August 3, 1944, though German propaganda reported that the factory was undamaged. The original classified U.S. Army report titled "Results at Manzell" tells another story:

> The factory has been devastated by a heavy and highly concentrated attack. Smoke was still rising from the battered remains of one building. The three primary targets have all been hit, among them the multifunctional shop is in ruins and the fitting and milling shop almost completely destroyed. Of six secondary objectives five have suffered severe damage and the rail road running along the rear of the factory has been cut at several points.[12]

The specific results of the mission were unknown to *Sugar Baby*'s crew. After the bomb release, their focus was on getting out of the area as quickly as possible. The flak had been heavy that morning but the fighter resistance they had expected was less so. The bombers flew another 30 kilometers and turned for home. My father looked down at his watch; it was 11:40 a.m. He had just crossed the German border and was flying directly over the Austrian Alps. He felt his tension ease, knowing the bombing mission had been successful. Although encountering heavier than usual flak over the factory in Friedrichshafen, they had managed to release their bombs effectively. Somehow, once again, they had survived. They had another mission under their belts and were one day closer to going home.

The mountains, at well over 6,000 feet in altitude, were snow-covered year round. There was low cloud cover, but the sun shone brightly and its reflection off the pure white snow was blinding at 19,000 feet. The serenity of magnificent mountains and clear blue skies calmed my father. *Sugar Baby* was on her way home and seemingly out of danger, but a new concern arose. A few B-24s in his box were faltering due to flak damage and began to lag behind. It was a cardinal rule that bombers were never to leave the main formation. It has not been determined who made the decision to hold back all six bombers for protection of the disabled aircraft. Debriefings months later pointed to the decision having been made by Lt. Crane. As all six planes were under his command, it would have been his direct order. Regardless, Charlie Box was falling behind.

The combined firepower of the bombers in Charlie Box, which included ten 50-caliber machine guns per ship, was a formidable opponent for attacking German fighters. The main formation was almost always escorted by American fighters and my father had grown to depend upon the presence of the P-51 Mustangs. He had noticed that part of their fighter support that morning was the Red Tail Angels. Flown by the famed Tuskegee Airmen, they were named for the easily recognized red tails and propellers of their aircraft. They were a great source of comfort to the bomber crews as they protectively buzzed around their formations. Their combat record consisted of a high kill ratio. More importantly, under their watch, very few Allied bombers were shot down by German fighters. The P-51 escort fighters were trained to stay with the main formation, forcing them to leave stray or damaged aircraft unattended. As the Liberators of Charlie Box fell further behind, they were joined by two more shrapnel-riddled bombers from a different box, and my father quickly realized there was not a P-51 in sight.

It was now 11:45 a.m. and he whispered a short prayer for everyone's safe return to base. Minutes later, 30 German fighters emerged from the clouds below and all hell broke loose. It was not until almost a full year later that the surviving crewmen were to learn exactly what had occurred that day. The combination of detailed records compiled by the Army Air Force concerning the air battle of August 3, 1944, and the invaluable debriefing of each crewman described the terrifying event. It was hard to believe that anyone survived the 30 seconds from the time the first 20mm shell tore open the Liberators' fuselages to the time they crashed and burned in the Austrian Alps.

As they approached the mountains, eight Liberators had been picked up by German radar. Me-109s and Fw-190s at a German air base nearby were alerted to the status of the weakened formation and ordered to attack. They had time to assemble groups of four to five fighters to overwhelm each American bomber. At 11:55 a.m., over the small village of Ehrwald, Austria, the German fighters attacked. The fight was vicious and one-sided. With four German fighters committed to each B-24, only one pass was needed to inflict mortal damage to all eight American aircraft. My dad and the other seventy-nine B-24 crewmen in his box never stood a chance.

During the raging battle, my father's body rocked as the starboard engine took a direct hit and was engulfed in flames. Exploding shells tore through *Sugar Baby*'s aluminum fuselage. Lt. Crane had already bailed out. Struggling at the controls, my dad realized that his efforts were futile and it would be impossible to save the aircraft.

The acrid smell of burning hydraulic fluid filled his nostrils, telling him what he already knew. Hydraulic lines had been shredded by enemy fighter machine gun bursts; without them there was no conceivable way to control the plane. Other smells attacked his senses and none of them were good. Burning fuel was everywhere and his eyes stung as the thick, black smoke enveloped him. The adrenaline emanating from crew members' pores acted like a pheromone, heightening the feeling of fear throughout the bomber. The worst by far was the stench that had my father's stomach churning. He recognized it immediately, the undeniable odor of burning flesh. He looked down at his pant leg and was shocked to see it on fire. A shard of shrapnel had torn through his calf and ignited parts of his uniform. As he ran down the catwalk, he suddenly stopped in his tracks; the entire tail of the B-24 was engulfed in flames. The tail gunner, Charlie Sellars, was lurching forward, his whole body on fire. With such severe injuries, he would not survive.

Unable to help him, my dad turned around and ran toward the bomb bay. Fire was now everywhere inside the fuselage and my father winced in pain as the flames from his burning bomber jacket singed his neck. He was bleeding from the shrapnel wound in his calf but there was no time to stanch the blood flow. The bomber was in a tailspin; there were only seconds left to bail out. Checking his parachute, he squeezed along the catwalk. Suddenly, he heard a cry for help from above. The top turret gunner's parachute cords were entangled in the torn metal of the fuselage and he was hopelessly stuck. Without a second thought, my father leapt towards Tony Jezowski, reached up, and successfully freed the cords. They both bailed out through the bomb bay doors, the last two men to exit the plane. Seconds later, *Sugar Baby* broke up in midair and crashed into the mountainside.

In less than a minute, eight American bombers had been shot out of the sky. In addition, eight German fighters were brought down by the Liberators' gunners, even though they had only seconds to react. The ensuing tally was horrifying. Of the 80 American crewmen, 30 were killed in action. Five German fighter pilots also perished that day. Forty-nine remaining American airmen, my father included, bailed out and were captured by the Germans. One member of my dad's crew was unaccounted for. Staff Sergeant Lawrence Hamilton's body was discovered two years later under the deep snow of the Austrian Alps.

Mercifully, my father cleared his burning bomber. He was aware that the time it took to untangle Jezowski while the bomber hurtled earthward had cost him precious seconds. He looked down in terror as the distance between him and the ground was gobbled up at a frightening rate. According to standards learned in training, the altitude at which his parachute deployed was well beneath the acceptable directive. But thankfully, it had opened and for a few brief moments he was suspended, drifting above the Alpine landscape. The quiet interlude was all too brief. Bullets started whizzing by his head as the German fighter pilots tried to clean up their handiwork. As he descended, my dad was threatened both by the strafing and the danger of his parachute catching fire or being struck by debris from the carnage of the planes falling from above. With only a few seconds left before touching down, the realization that he had survived the bloodshed in the skies above humbled him. Although it had been his first jump, it had gone surprisingly well, and he landed softly in a meadow, with only a few additional scrapes and bruises.

My father's mind immediately went into a practical mode. He disposed of his parachute and his 45-caliber firearm, knowing he would undoubtedly be killed if found in possession of a weapon. The loss of blood from his shrapnel wound was beginning to weaken him. He was experiencing light-headedness and it troubled him; he knew he would need all his faculties to formulate some type of survival plan. As he looked down into the emerald valley below, seeing cows and goats lazily grazing, the thought struck him that less than an hour before, the entire area must have been beautiful. Now it was strewn with tangled bodies of men and machines.

My father lay bleeding in the grass, and thoughts of Peggy and Bobby raced through his mind. He vowed to make it back home alive...somehow, some way. Training had taught him that it was a distinct possibility that German soldiers or possibly even civilians might kill him. He knew the enemy was already scouring the mountains and valleys for surviving American airmen.

As my father walked over the last knoll into the valley, he realized that his leg wound required immediate medical attention. Hiding would be senseless. He noticed a woman with two young children picnicking in the meadow. Their presence seemed surreal after what had transpired only minutes before. Suddenly, three German soldiers appeared out of nowhere, running directly at him, guns drawn. My father raised his arms in surrender, but the Germans ignored the gesture and began to beat him with their weapons and their fists. He prayed that it would not be his fate to die in that field, halfway across the world.

He had one last hope. He remembered the last time he was with Peggy before shipping overseas—they had formed a plan. They each decided to keep a baby slipper of Bobby's with them at all times, a concrete symbol of the hope that my father would return home safely and the slippers would become a pair once again. He reached inside his bomber jacket for the slipper, pulled it out and showed it to his attackers, hoping that one or more of the men beating him might be a father and understand it to be poignant proof of a child he had back home. It was a desperate move but it saved his life. Within seconds of seeing that baby slipper, the German guards lowered their guns and fists, the assault ended, and my father became a prisoner of the Third Reich.

CAPTIVITY

I T WAS LATE AFTERNOON ON AUGUST 3, 1944. THE QUAINT mountain inn located on the grassy meadows of the Ehrwalder Alm at the base of the Alps in Ehrwald, Austria, was filling up with people. On any given day, hikers and picnickers would stop by the inn for a bite to eat or a cold drink. Today, however, was different. The people sandwiched into the tiny confines of the inn were not revelers. They were American airmen, some injured, all exhausted, all scared. The late summer heat was oppressive, and the crowded conditions offered no relief. A picture of Adolph Hitler covered one entire wall. In an e-mail sent to me 60 years later, Gerd Leitner noted, "Looking at that wall confirmed one thing for the American airmen. They sure weren't in Switzerland!"

My father's leg throbbed, although he had been able to slow the blood flow from his shrapnel wound. Orders were given for the German guards to round up the prisoners and march them to the train station at the center of the village. My dad was concerned about his fellow crewmen from *Sugar Baby*. Since watching them bail out, he had not seen anyone. His thoughts were interrupted as a German soldier bellowed, "Raus!" The path down from the valley to the village was a few miles long and, for many of the injured airmen, the trek was torturous. Injuries ranged from bumps and bruises to severe lacerations, life-threatening burns, and broken limbs. After taking care of their own casualties, the German and Austrian doctors tended to the critically injured Americans. For a few of the severely wounded airmen, the last breath they would take would be in a tiny Austrian village, thousands of miles from home.

My dad's wound was not life-threatening. The doctors cleaned the shrapnel hole that had torn through his calf and packed it with sulfa powder to fight infection. The lack of painkillers still left him uncomfortable, but the bleeding had stopped. He was marched to the local police station where he saw George, Joe, and Lt. Crane. They quickly huddled together, but before anyone had a chance to say anything, a German guard broke them up. They were herded toward the local train station where rail cars awaited to take them to the town of Garmisch. With the mass confusion, my father became separated from his fellow crewmen and eventually he lost sight of them.

The German soldiers wasted no time loading the prisoners on the train. My father welcomed the opportunity to sit down and rest his injured leg. It was late evening and he felt safer on the train than among the local crowd that had gathered at the station. The mood of the villagers had originally been one of curiosity, but at the sight of the hated Americans in their town, it quickly transformed into one of hostility. As my dad peered through the train window, he realized he was staring at a jeering mob. They were screaming in German; he didn't need a translator to understand their intent. My father had been taught in training to fear the civilians even more than the German guards. By August of 1944, almost all of them had had at least one family member killed or injured in the war and they took every chance to exact revenge on their enemy. A number of British and American prisoners were killed by the locals before they ever reached the German prison camps. He looked into the eyes of the crazed crowd and silently prayed for God's protection.

As the train left the Ehrwald station, my father, although surrounded by fellow prisoners, felt entirely alone. He had no idea what his destination was or how long it would take to get there. From his training in the States, he was acutely aware that interrogation was imminent and it scared the hell out of him. Stories of torture and endless days spent in solitary confinement abounded. My dad shuddered at the thought of being trapped inside a narrow room with no windows or light, and he felt his heart pounding in his chest. The fear of never seeing his wife or son again drained him. He had made a vow to himself to return to them safely and he was determined to honor it. Exhausted by the horrific events of the day, my father fell into a deep sleep.

The screeching brakes of the train arriving in Garmisch jolted him awake. Sleep had provided him a brief escape, but now the reality set in that he was a prisoner of war. German guards stood, guns drawn, at each end of the rail car. At their order, the American prisoners rose to their feet and were paraded off the train in single file. Even though it was now almost midnight, the air was still and the heat of the August day had not dissipated. My father fell in line and was careful to stay close to the airman in front of him; because of the mandatory blackout, there was no lighting to help them find their way. His leg began to throb again as they were marched through Garmisch. Fortunately, it was not long before they came to a large three-story white brick building that appeared to be some type of small fortress. It was a German military facility that housed their mountain division troops.

The prisoners were led inside and were relieved to find many of their comrades already there. My dad noticed a small group of airmen in the far corner of the room and although they were facing away from him, he was pretty sure that he recognized the voices of George Britton and Joe Spontak. His assumption was confirmed as they turned around to greet him. He was overjoyed to be reunited with his boys. Joe, George, Pat Logan, and Lt. Crane were all there. They anxiously whispered among themselves.

"Where the hell did those Jerries come from?"

"Did you see Jack Favier's ship take a direct hit? Nobody could have lived through that!"

"Yeah, I only saw three chutes coming from Fiecoat's plane; it didn't look good."

The first question for any bomber crew was how many parachutes were seen leaving their aircraft before it either exploded in mid-air or crashed. Answers varied, but most agreed only nine out of ten chutes had escaped *Sugar Baby* as she hurtled downward. They sadly nodded in agreement discussing the fate of their replacement tail gunner, Charlie Sellars; he appeared mortally wounded as a result of direct hits on his position from the German fighters' deadly cannons. My father was not the only one of the crew with injuries. Joe's were relatively minor: he had some teeth knocked loose when the buckle of his parachute whipped back into his face. George's were more serious: a few shards of shrapnel had embedded in his armpit and his shoulder had taken quite a jolt when his parachute violently swung into a tree. All in all, they had come out of the air battle relatively unscathed. As a group, they could only conjure up wild theories as to what might lay ahead for them in the next few days.

As it turned out, their first week of captivity was relatively quiet. On the first night, they had been ordered upstairs to a set of rooms that were vacant due to a mass deployment of the German Mountain Division stationed there. They were ordered to leave the doors to their rooms open at all times and were allowed to talk to each other. The men were taken outside to a field across the street from their building for an hour of exercise twice a day. My father's leg was getting better and he looked forward to this daily ritual, if for no other reason than the chance to get some fresh air. For the most part, the food was tolerable. Their German captors did not question them at all during their stay; each man was well aware that when the order came to move out of this building, their next stop would be the dreaded Dulag Luft Interrogation Center. The respite was short-lived. After a few days, the Germans issued the order to evacuate. My dad, Lt. Crane, Pat, George, and Joe gathered one last time to wish each other luck and say their goodbyes. Once on the train to Dulag Luft, there was a distinct possibility they would never see each other again.

As the American airmen boarded the train, my father noted that once again there were only two German guards per car. They displayed no animosity towards their prisoners; my father had expected much worse. As he gazed out the window, a commotion caught his eye. German soldiers in black uniforms, accompanied by menacing guard dogs, were herding a group of men and women into a rail car normally used for transporting livestock. All of them wore black and white striped baggy clothes. Unlike the guards in his car, these soldiers physically abused their prisoners. The sheer number of men and women being squeezed into the livestock car defied belief. They stood, elbow to elbow, not allowed to sit down. With the boxcar filled to an inhumane capacity, its doors were closed. My dad wondered what they had possibly done to deserve such brutal treatment. It wasn't until after the war's end that he would discover the horrifying truth. The striped-clad men and women had been Jews.

The heat inside my father's rail car was rising. He was alone with his thoughts. George, Joe, Lt. Crane, and Pat were in different cars; my dad had lost sight of them earlier. The Americans were ordered not to speak among themselves, and my father found himself already missing the camaraderie he had shared with *Sugar Baby*'s officers while in Garmisch; the silence in the car was deafening. As the train pulled out of the station, he shivered with fear despite the insufferable heat; the bile rose in his throat as his thoughts focused on his next destination: Dulag Luft.

Dulag Luft is the abbreviated term for *Durchgangslager der Luftwaffe*. In English, it meant "entrance camp" or "transit camp" of the Air Force.[1] Located in Oberursel, Germany, just north of Frankfurt and about 300 miles from Garmisch, it was the premier interrogation center for Allied airmen shot down over Europe. Only airmen shot down over Italy had a different clearing center; their Dulag Luft was in Verona, Italy. With only a few British and French prisoners of war, the interrogation facility at Oberursel began its operation in December of 1939, in what was known as the "Stonehouse."[2] As war escalated, so did the number of prisoners, and in 1940, three additional wooden barracks were erected to accommodate the captured airmen, with the Stonehouse becoming the primary interrogation building. The number of Allied airmen that passed through Oberursel per year increased at a staggering rate for the next three years: 3,000 in 1942; 8,000 in 1943; and an incredible 29,000 in 1944.[3]

Dulag Luft's staff consisted of 25 to 30 English-fluent Luftwaffe officers for detailed interrogation, and 15 to 18 officers for preliminary interrogation.[4] Training in the States had taught my father what to expect upon arriving there. Solitary confinement was the primary tactic used to mentally and physically wear down the prisoners prior to interrogation. My dad knew to reveal only his name, rank, and serial number. He was also aware that the Germans would use every available method to obtain additional information. Hundreds of miles still remained before he would reach Oberursel. The rhythmic click-clack of the railway was lulling him to sleep and he welcomed its cadence.

My father awoke drenched in sweat. A cacophony of bombs exploding had shocked him out of a deep sleep. Now wide awake, he was trying to identify a different noise; it was a sharp ping of metal on metal and he knew he had heard it somewhere before. "My God," he thought, "we're being strafed by our own guys!" The next few minutes were nerve-wracking. It was a very real possibility that he might have survived the air battle only to be killed on a train by friendly fire. Then, as quickly as it had started, it was over. Everyone in his car was unharmed; he wondered about the boys from *Sugar Baby* in the other cars. He couldn't fault the Allied fighter pilots because many of their primary targets were railway lines and trains. With no possible way to know which ones were transporting American prisoners, they attacked them all with a vengeance. In contrast, Dad remembered learning that the Dulag Luft buildings were safe from being bombed by Allied forces because "POW" had been painted in huge white letters on the top of the facility and on all the large boulders around the perimeter.[5]

The remainder of the trip to Frankfurt was uneventful. A couple of nights were spent in German jails; it was a harbinger of what awaited them in Dulag Luft. No one had bathed in days; the stench of body odor was overwhelming in the tight confines of their rail car. My father was thirsty and hungry every waking minute. Meals consisted of black bread partially made from sawdust, perhaps a piece of moldy cheese, and the infamous blood sausage that gagged him as he gulped it down. He realized they were already becoming animals in order to survive. Closing his eyes, he hoped that sleep would take his mind off the emptiness gnawing at his gut.

He awoke to the noise of another angry mob; they had arrived in Frankfurt. The prisoners were ordered off the train, sticking close to the German guards as they waited on a platform for the half-hour tram ride to the town of Oberursel. Frankfurt citizens surrounded the airmen and began to move in. The crowd's cries of "baby killers" and "murderers" echoed through the rail station. The minute the tram arrived, the airmen crammed themselves into the trolley, thankful to be away from the agitated horde.

As they pulled into Oberursel, my father took in the surrounding area, noting that three sets of buildings composed the Dulag Luft compound: Auswertestelle West, which was the interrogation center, the Hohe-Mark Hospital, and the Wetzlar, which was the transit camp and the last stop for the prisoners before being shipped out to their permanent prisoner of war camps. From his training, he immediately recognized a U-shaped building. Known as the cooler, it was the most feared facility of the complex. The cooler meant only one thing—solitary confinement.[6]

The walk to the white building at the entrance to Dulag Luft gave my father a welcome chance to stretch his legs after days spent on the cramped train. My father needed to get news to Peggy that he was okay, and that everything would be all right, even as he more fervently wanted to believe it himself. Thinking about home, he knew the dreaded "missing in action" telegram would soon arrive in White Plains. He imagined Peggy seeing a Western Union delivery boy parking his bike at the curb and holding her breath as he came to her door to deliver the heart-stopping news. She would open it to read:

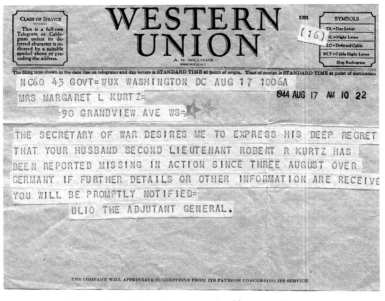

Missing in Action telegram received by Peggy Kurtz,
fourteen days after her husband, Bob, was shot down

Article in White Plains local newspaper,
The Reporter Dispatch, August 1944

TWO CITY AIRMEN MISSING IN ACTION

Kurtz, Grace Are Reported Downed Over Europe; Valhalla Marine Wounded

Two White Plains men have been reported missing over Europe, and a Valhalla Marine has been wounded in action, according to information issued by the War Department.

Second Lieutenant Robert R. Kurtz, son of Mr. and Mrs. Russell Kurtz, 25 Cushman Road, has been missing over Germany since Aug. 3. Co-pilot of a Liberator bomber, he was on his 19th mission at the time. He was stationed at an air base in Italy.

Lieutenant Kurtz is a graduate of White Plains High School and attended Bowdoin College and New York University. His wife, the former Margaret Luther, and their son, Robert R. Kurtz, Jr., live with her parents, Mr. and Mrs. Ward L. Luther, 90 Grandview Avenue.

Upon entering the white building, my father was led to a room and strip-searched. Soon afterward, his clothes were returned; he was photographed and fingerprinted. Second Lt. Robert R. Kurtz, co-pilot, U.S. Army Air Force, was now officially a prisoner of war.

Having completed the intake procedure, a German guard led my dad down a long corridor to the cooler. All 240 cells were identical: five feet by twelve feet, and eight feet high, with a cot, a table, a wooden chair, and an electric bell to call a guard.[7] The only source of light was a ceiling bulb that seldom worked. The bathroom facilities were located at the end of the hall and prisoners were at the full mercy of the guards when they needed to relieve themselves. They would find out that one of the ploys used in interrogation was the promise of more bathroom privileges with the release of additional information beyond their simple name, rank, and serial number. For the prisoners who refused that offer, their remaining option was to push a red flag through a slot in the door and hope a guard would acknowledge it.

As he entered his cell, my father's heart sank when he saw that there was only one window, and it was painted black. He sat down on his cot and before the guard had closed the cell door, there was just enough light to see fleas hopping back and forth on his mattress. In spots there were so many, they had turned the gray mattress black. When the cell door slammed shut, he was faced with the finality of his situation. Alone, in an unbearably hot, dark cell, with fleas that were already feasting on his body, he wondered how he could possibly survive.

A couple of hours later, he heard the key turn. A German military officer disguised in civilian clothes entered and escorted my dad to an interrogation room, where he handed him a Red Cross form and told him to fill it out in full. The first three questions were the inevitable name, rank, and serial number. They were followed by questions of a personal nature: information about spouses, children, and addresses. If he supplied the personal information, the Germans would guarantee prompt notification to his next of kin that he was alive and well. The next few lines were military questions. My father was told if he answered these, solitary confinement time would be reduced. The Germans wanted squadron numbers, air base locations, types of aircraft flown, and most importantly, bombing mission locations. Once again, his training proved invaluable. He knew that the form in his hands was bogus. Why would the Red Cross need to know the whereabouts of his bombing missions? The interrogators, once armed with information supplied by the prisoners, could break them down mentally, especially after a few days in the cooler. He took the pen from the "civilian," filled out the first three lines, and promptly handed it back. The man became irate and threatened my father with endless days in solitary. Once again, my dad refused and was taken back to his cell.

Now alone with his thoughts, he hoped he had done the right thing. Due to his growing hunger, the interrogator had come close to breaking him with the promise of Red Cross parcels filled with food and cigarettes. He curled up on the cement floor in the corner of his cell, not wanting any part of the flea-infested mattress. His last thoughts before lapsing into a fatigue-induced sleep were the same as they had been every night—thoughts of home and family.

The next three days of solitary confinement proved to be some of the worst of his life, but the daily, hour-long interrogation process was easier than he had expected. Each day, my dad was led into a room and questioned by a German officer fluent in English, whose job was to obtain information by befriending him. The amount of knowledge the officer had about my father's family, squadron, and their missions was unnerving, and he wondered which of his fellow airmen had collapsed under the pressures of interrogation. He stood fast and never offered more than the basic details described in Article 17 of the Geneva Convention, the classic "name, rank, and serial number."[8] He didn't know at the time that his unwillingness to talk would, surprisingly, result in a shorter stay in Dulag Luft. In 1944, 3,000 airmen were processed through the center each month. At times, four to five men occupied a cell meant for one prisoner. Consequently, the Germans ended interrogation after three days for prisoners who would not cooperate.[9] The men who had been mentally broken and could potentially provide additional intelligence were kept longer.

The interrogation was difficult, but it was the other 23 hours of the day that sapped my dad's strength. The August heat was brutal; with no trees around the facility, the cells baked in the afternoon sun and reeked of the prisoners' perspiration. The constant itching of flea bites drove him crazy. Meals consisted of watery sauerkraut soup and tasteless German black bread. One night he discovered a worm in his soup and was shocked at how greedily he devoured it. But it was the darkness that was the real killer...the darkness and the solitude. As a pilot, he had always been in control; now he had no control over his life whatsoever.

After three days and nights in the cooler, he had reached his wit's end. The fourth morning began with the familiar clank of the guard's key. He had come to welcome the sound; it meant that, for at least an hour, he would be free from his solitary cell. But this day was different. As they approached the door to the interrogation room, my father realized that the guard was not slowing down. Shortly thereafter, the exterior door to the cooler was opened; his three days of hell were finally over. He welcomed the blinding midday sun and sucked in huge gulps of fresh air. Even the sight of more German soldiers didn't upset him; isolation had clearly taken its toll.

His next stop was the Wetzlar transit camp. It was there that German officers determined which prisoner of war camp each airman would be assigned to. The prisoners were given back some of their personal items that had been confiscated days earlier.[10] The Germans had taken the men's bomber jackets and boots, which they kept for themselves. My father was thankful that they returned his wedding ring, watch, and Bobby's baby slipper. Each prisoner was supplied with a Red Cross capture kit. This was a cardboard suitcase with the Red Cross emblem imprinted on it. Inside were fresh under-wear, socks, cigarettes, toiletries, a shirt, a pair of pants, a wool cap, gloves, and an Army field jacket. More important than creature comforts, the captives were allowed to send one telegram back home.[11] On August 13, 1944, my dad wired:

> MY DARLING—AM SAFE, WELL AND COM-PLETELY UNHARMED. WILL BE AT PERMA-NENT PRISON CAMP VERY SOON AND WILL BE ABLE TO WRITE YOU LETTERS FROM THERE. DON'T WRITE ADDRESS ON FRONT. I THINK OF YOU AND BOBBY EVERY SECOND— IT WON'T BE VERY LONG, HONEY, I PROMISE ... DON'T WORRY AND TAKE REAL GOOD CARE OF YOURSELF—I ADORE YOU. PLEASE TELL FOLKS. I LOVE YOU. BOB

The Germans determined that my father was to be held as a prisoner of war in Stalag Luft III, located in Sagan, Germany, 100 miles southeast of Berlin. It was the first of several camps that my father would endure. The prisoners were usually transported in large groups. On August 13, 1944, my dad and fellow airmen left Oberursel for Sagan. The train ride lasted three days. The closer they got to Berlin, the more they feared for their lives; constant bombing and strafing of the train by Allied planes grated on their nerves. Once again, tight confinement, intense heat, and hunger all contributed to a miserable journey. But most of all, for my father as well as for all the airmen bound for Stalag Luft III, the reality of their situation was setting in. In three days they would be prisoners of war in a permanent camp.

On the third day, as the prisoners' train slowed to a stop, my father looked out on what had once been a beautiful city. Berlin, heart of the Third Reich, thought to be impenetrable to the Allied assault, lay in bombed-out ruins. The city was a hollowed-out shell of what had once been a symbol of power. My dad could feel a smile forming on his face, his first in God knows how many days, because the fall of Germany's capital would clearly shorten the war in Europe, thus offering him a chance to get home sooner. He immediately chastised himself because his smile was a selfish one. He had been entertaining thoughts of being home by Christmas, but now he became aware of the enormous loss of human lives. It was August 16, 1944, and as the train left a battered Berlin on its way to Stalag Luft III, he gazed out at the carnage that brutal carpet bombings had inflicted on the once-majestic city. Everywhere, men, women, and children lay dead in the streets, their lifeless forms bent grotesquely at incomprehensible angles, and he had to wonder if the end had justified the means. His heart was heavy, knowing that the people he had seen lying in the streets were simply innocent victims of a savage war. They would never see another Christmas.

The 100-mile train ride took a little over three hours. Sagan was located in Upper Silesia, once known as Prussia. The POW camp's location had been predetermined. The word "Silesia" translates to "sand," the primary ingredient of Stalag Luft III's soil.[12] Acutely aware that the prisoners were intent on escaping by tunneling out of the compound, the Germans picked the site knowing that the loosely grained sand would make it virtually impossible to shore up a tunnel's wall. That's not saying it couldn't be done. A few months prior to my father's arrival, 76 prisoners had tunneled out of the camp—a feat that was later featured in the book and movie, *The Great Escape*. Although most of the men were caught within days, their exploits left a black mark on the camp's reputation. Upon notification of the escape, Adolph Hitler ordered 50 of the recaptured men to be shot.[13] German officers in command of Stalag Luft III were sharply reprimanded; the commandant was court-martialed. Due to the magnitude and notoriety of the escape, the prisoner of war camp my father was about to enter had heightened its security considerably. Tighter control brought with it harsher treatment for the prisoners and fewer privileges. Totally unaware of the events that had preceded his arrival and of how they would affect his imprisonment, my father exited the train and began the short march to Stalag Luft III.

The majestic pine trees that lined the sandy lane leading to the camp emitted an intoxicating smell, reminding my dad of long hikes he had taken through the Adirondack Mountains back home, a home that seemed so far away now. As he gazed into the cobalt-blue skies above the trees, he prayed for God's guidance and protection.

A few minutes later, my father's admiration of his surroundings was harshly interrupted. The prisoners rounded a final bend in the road and were staring at a formidable sight. Ten-foot-high stockade fences, looming guard towers, and ferocious guard dogs stood only yards away. The flag of the Third Reich with its spider-like swastika waved ominously from its tall flagpole. The enormous front gate swung open with a loud groan and my dad and his fellow prisoners were led inside. Moments later, the creaking of the gate was followed by a noise my father would never forget—the sound of the huge doors slamming shut. From that point on, he was officially a *kriegie*, a shortened version of the German word *kriegsgefangener*: prisoner of war.[14]

Guard towers manned by German soldiers armed with rifles were strategically placed inside the compound, each one fitted with a powerful searchlight able to cover every inch of the camp's perimeters at night. Barbed wire was everywhere; its menacing, jagged steel points shone like daggers in the late summer sun. Once again, he felt out of control and helpless, realizing that this bleak encampment would be his home for at least the next few months.

Among the magical contents of the green box that I discovered as a child, there was a typewritten sheet that contained quotes from the book, *My Early Life*, by Winston Churchill. As a young boy, I had passed over it quickly, much more interested in the medals, pictures, and letters that were part of my father's life. Now, almost 60 years later, the fact that my dad took the time to type out excerpts of Churchill's book provides me with a huge insight into my father's thoughts about the imprisonment that wore him down daily. Churchill, a prisoner of war during the Boer War, wrote:

> You are in the power of your enemy. You owe your life to his humanity and your daily bread to his compassion. You must obey his orders, go where he tells you, stay where you are bid, await his pleasure, possess your soul in patience. The days are very long, hours crawl by like paralytic centipedes. Nothing amuses you, reading is difficult, writing impossible. Life is one long boredom from dawn to slumber. The whole atmosphere of prison is odious. If you have never been under restraint before, and never known what it was to be a captive, you feel a sense of constant humiliation in being confined to a narrow space, fenced in by wire, watched by armed guards, and webbed in by a tangle of regulations.[15]

My father was led into a bare-walled building where he again was fingerprinted, photographed, and strip-searched. The odor of unwashed bodies was overpowering in the tiny room. Most of these men had not bathed in weeks, if not months; the opportunity to finally take a shower made them feel human for the first time in a long time. Before dressing in the clothes provided by the Red Cross, the prisoners were dusted for lice and fleas. They were then issued a metal kriegie dog tag with a POW number stamped on it; my dad's was #7241. Once outside the cramped building, he got the first real glimpse of his new world.

Stalag Luft III was operated by the Luftwaffe. Built primarily for British RAF and American Air Force officers, it consisted of several compounds. The first compound built, which opened in March 1942, was designated the East Compound; its prisoners were mainly British Royal Air Force officers. The Center Compound opened in

April 1942, and while originally built for British sergeants, it became a facility for Americans by the end of the year. In March of 1943, the North Compound was erected and housed British airmen. The South Compound, built in September 1943, was followed by the West Compound in July 1944; both were constructed for American officers, whose numbers had overtaken the British prisoners' dramatically. The compounds were filling up at an alarming rate and by 1944, both British and American airmen were housed wherever there was a vacancy.[16] My father was taken to the North Compound where he found almost 90 percent of the men to be British.

Before going inside his barracks, he observed the surrounding buildings. Each compound had 15 single-story barracks that contained ten-foot by twelve-foot bunkrooms; each bunkroom slept 15 men in five triple-decker bunks. At capacity in late 1944, Stalag Luft III housed 2,500 RAF officers, 7,500 USAAF officers and another 1,000 Allied officers of different nationalities. The total was a staggering 11,000 prisoners in a camp built for half that number.[17]

When my dad entered his barracks, he encountered a group of Brits talking animatedly among themselves. However, when he approached them, their conversation stopped. He tried to introduce himself but was ignored. None of the RAF officers made any attempt to welcome him. Instead, two of the men pulled my father back outside and began walking with him around the compound. When finally he was recognized by two other prisoners, probably airmen from the 465th Bomb Group, they loosened their grip on my father's arms and introduced themselves. Only after verifying his identity did they let my dad know why he had been given the silent treatment. German infiltrators who spoke perfect English were a threat to the prisoners. Discussions of tunnel escape plans were common in every barracks; they could not afford a spy among them, so they devised a simple plan. Newcomers to the camp had to be personally vouched for by two existing POWs who knew the prisoner by sight. If he failed the sight recognition, he was constantly interrogated by fellow prisoners and accompanied everywhere outside the barracks. This system worked to perfection—no infiltrator was ever successful at Stalag Luft III.[18]

The two RAF officers brought my father back to the barracks and everyone was introduced. My dad immediately took a liking to his bunkmates from across the pond. Nevertheless, friendship had its bounds. Being the newcomer, he was automatically low man on the totem pole. The Brits good-naturedly gestured to the top bed of the three-tiered bunk, letting him know, in no uncertain terms, that it was exclusively his. My father noticed that quite a few of the wooden slats were missing from beneath his mattress. His fellow prisoners explained they had been used to shore up walls in one of three tunnels currently being dug. It was at that point that my dad knew that if asked to help in the digging of the tunnels, he would decline. It wasn't because he didn't support their efforts and he certainly understood their compulsion to escape. Although he did take turns as a lookout for escape efforts, my father's primary concern was to get home safely to his family, something he would not jeopardize for anything. Other prisoners had told him that men who had been caught tunneling had been shot; it just wasn't worth it.

When my father entered Stalag Luft III, he was issued a knife, fork, spoon, cup, and bowl, each etched with a black swastika on the handle.[19] Aware that the prisoners might attempt to use them as tunneling tools, the German guards regularly took stock of the utensils, making sure all were there and letting them know that if any were lost, they would not be replaced. As far as meals went, my dad was disgusted to find out that the menu at Stalag Luft III mirrored that of Dulag Luft. One change was for the worse; the sauerkraut soup with a worm floating in it that he had eaten the previous week was replaced by the infamous "green death soup." This was a concoction of water, green weeds, dehydrated vegetables, and often, even more worms. The quality of the water alone was questionable; outbreaks of diarrhea, dysentery, and occasionally diphtheria ran rampant throughout the camp. Some of the men suffered with intestinal ailments for the rest of their lives. The notorious black bread was a staple in the kriegie diet. Although he was famished, my father stared down at his first meal in Stalag Luft III. One of the main ingredients of the bread was sawdust, which made its taste and texture almost unpalatable. He noticed other prisoners dunking their bread into the green death soup; when saturated, they were able to force it down. Knowing he had to eat to survive, he followed suit. A few hours later, it was time for evening roll call. Immediately afterwards, exhausted from the day's events, my father climbed into his top bunk and was sound asleep in seconds.

SPECIAL TREAT
BLACK BREAD
BROAT RECIPE
Former prisoners of war of Nazi Germany may be interested in this recipe for WWII Black Bread. This recipe comes from the official record from the food providing ministry published (top secret) Berlin 24.XI 1941 and the Director in Ministry Herr Mansfeld and Herr Moritz. It was agreed that the best mixture to bake Black Bread was:
50% bruised rye grain
20% sliced sugar beets
20% tree flour (sawdust)
10% minced leaves
and straw
From our own experiences with the Black Bread, we also saw bits of glass and sand. Someone was cheating on the recipe!
Joseph P. O'Donnell[20]

He awoke the next morning with the identical thought he would awake with each morning for the duration of his captivity—the thought of Peggy, Bobby, his parents, and home. It was essential that he let them know he was okay. Borrowing some stationery from a bunkmate, he sat down to write his first letter home; it was August 17, 1944:

My own dearest one, I'm permanently located now, darling, and very comfortable. We live in barracks, have plenty of food and clothes, and are much better off than I hoped for. At present I'm with some English boys who have been grand to me. I hope and pray with all my heart that it didn't take long for you to receive the telegram saying that I was alive and safe. I've been able to think of nothing else since we were shot down, I know how tough it must have been for you not knowing. Things are going so well, dearest, it can't be very long till I'm home with you and Bobby and this time for our 75 years. I can't wait to hear from you, it'll take several months, they say. Please don't stop things at home, baby. I spend every waking moment right there with you, and am perfectly OK. They let me keep Bobby's slipper. Please send a snap in your letter of you and Bobby, I have none. I adore you my darling. Your very own, Bob.

Shortly after, on August 22, 1944, he wrote to his parents:

> *Dearest Folks, After being shot down by fighters over Germany Aug 3 and bailing out safely, I'm now very well settled at this camp with some British fellows— completely well and unharmed. The facilities here are remarkable—the Red Cross can give you all the details concerning this particular camp. We all feel that we'll be home soon. So save me some Thanksgiving turkey. Don't worry, I'm fine. All my love, Bob.*

All things considered, my father was being relatively honest in his letters home concerning conditions at Stalag Luft III. The camp was operated by the Luftwaffe, led by Hermann Göring. In the hierarchy of German command, Göring was second in rank and answered only to Adolf Hitler.[21] He respected all airmen officers, whether they were allies or enemies, and treated them accordingly. He ordered the camp's guards, as well as its officers, to comply with the terms of the Geneva Convention, using force only when necessary.

Stalag Luft III offered the best organized recreational facilities of any POW camp in Germany.[22] It had athletic fields as well as courts for basketball and volleyball. The prisoners organized teams, set up schedules, and engaged in friendly competition to earn bragging rights and best team honors. It was a great way to break the boredom of everyday kriegie life and also blow off a little steam. My father enjoyed competition and had been very athletic in his pre-war years. However, at Stalag Luft III, he lost interest in sports. He exercised daily, but the idea of joining teams was unappealing. Football and basketball reminded my father of life back in the States. As each day of captivity crawled on, memories of those games reminded him how far away from home he really was.

My dad fully understood how important it was to be active during the long days. One of his bunkmates chose to stay inside the barracks, only leaving for mandatory roll calls or to use the latrine. My father watched daily as the man lay still in his bunk. He rarely spoke, but when he did, he related stories of life in his beloved Great Britain. The fellow talked about his wife and young daughter and how positive he was he would never see them again. He wept frequently and my dad realized that despair was slowly killing him. Looking at the woeful Brit, my dad was determined the same would not happen to him.

Since he had decided that organized sports would not be an option, my father chose to exercise his mind instead. The library at Stalag Luft III was extensive, with books supplied by the YMCA accounting for most of the inventory. Incredibly, the kriegies were allowed to take courses in foreign language, law, or engineering. By attending classes, studying, and passing exams supplied by the Red Cross, they could earn their degrees.[24] My father was not interested in a degree, but he was an avid reader and he utilized the library's facilities daily. In a postcard to his parents dated August 28, 1944, he wrote:

> *Dearest Folks, All is going fine. I've been splitting my days into about ½ sunshine and exercise and ½ reading. This past week I read 3 biographies—Shakespeare, John Wesley, and Audubon. They have a very good library here and of course we have plenty of time to read. I'm curious to know if anything came of my article. Sure would love some mail but guess that will be months yet. Take care of yourselves. Lots of love, Bob.*

In his letter, he mentioned his essay, "Twenty-Four Hours of Flight." While at Pantanella, my dad had worked on it every possible minute. He wrote a letter to his father telling him he was sick of reading it over and over, but he wanted it to be perfect. My grandfather was an editor with literary connections that my dad hoped would enable him to get his piece published. With hours upon hours of unending boredom, his repeated review of his story while at Pantanella had enabled him to memorize it in full. My father recreated it in his head every day, using it as a form of mental exercise.

The next few weeks were tedious. My father learned the lay of the land in his compound and was getting accustomed to the daily monotony of kriegie life. He was starting to feel the physical effects of captivity. He was losing weight; the bread and soup were barely edible and never enough. Even though their delivery was unpredictable, my dad and his fellow prisoners depended on shipments of Red Cross parcels arriving at Stalag Luft III. Each parcel weighed about 11 pounds and contained items specifically designed to supply nutrition and valuable elements that were lacking in the prisoners' diets. Typical British Red Cross parcels provided small tins of tea, chocolate, pudding, cheese, condensed milk, dried eggs, margarine, vegetables, biscuits, cocoa powder and some type of meat roll. Nonedible items included a bar of soap and cigarettes.[23] The packages were distributed equally among the prisoners; the Germans were surprisingly good about not hoarding them. For the starving prisoners, arrival of Red Cross parcels was a huge morale booster. There was only one thing better—mail from home. Although my mother and his parents wrote him almost every day, mail delivery to and from the ETO (European Theater of Operations) was agonizingly slow. It was not uncommon for a letter to take six months to arrive at the German POW camps. My father was never in any camp more than five months and the Germans were in no rush to forward correspondence. The lack of news from home was a key factor contributing to his depression through the long months of imprisonment.

That's not to say that there weren't some lighter moments in kriegie life. The prisoners had come to know the 800 German guards at Stalag Luft III very well. Each compound had one or two guards everyone knew to steer clear of, but for the most part, the Germans and the prisoners were civil to one another. The prisoners called their guards "goons." My father's bunkmates explained why the Germans were not angered by this apparent insult. They were told, and actually believed, that the word "goon" was an abbreviated form of "German Officers Or Non-coms."[25] My dad smiled every time one of his fellow prisoners would summon a guard over to their barracks and say something like, "The goon wants to know if you have any extra cigarettes." It was a constant source of amusement for the men. Another enjoyable prisoner pastime that frustrated the guards no end was played out at morning and evening roll call. American and British officers would purposely line up out of order, switch names with each other, or change positions in line and be counted more than once. It confounded the guards, and their morning and evening roll call numbers would always be off.

It was mid-September, more than six weeks since he had been shot down, and he continually wondered if Peggy had been notified of whether or not he was alive. My dad wouldn't know until after the war that a telegram dated September 6, 1944, had arrived at her parents' home, where she and Bobby were living and anxiously awaiting news. It read:

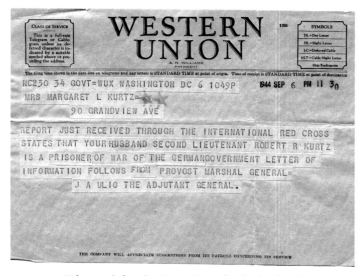

Telegram informing Peggy Kurtz that her husband
is alive and a prisoner of war

The days between the missing in action telegram she received dated August 17, 1944, and the above telegram, a period of almost three weeks, were incredibly hard for my mother. This was her first notification that he was alive. The letters my dad had written from Dulag Luft and Stalag Luft III would not arrive until months later. The weeks of not knowing whether he was alive or dead would have been unbearable for my mom if not for the loving support of her parents and the comfort that Bobby brought her.

Once she had received her telegram from the Red Cross, my mother and the relatives of the remaining crew members of *Sugar Baby* set up a network of communication. In a letter dated December 12, 1944, that I obtained from Debbie Beson, daughter of *Sugar Baby* gunner Tony Jezowski, my mother wrote:

> *Dear Mr. and Mrs. Jezowski, I received a letter from the War Department with the names of the boys on my husband's crew and their next of kin. I have gotten several letters from different families with the in-*

*formation that their sons are prisoners, and one still
missing. I have been fortunate in being one of those
with my husband a prisoner, and am so anxious to
know whether you have heard as yet. Perhaps you too
have heard some details. If so, I would appreciate any
news as every little bit helps as you know. If I learn
anything further, I shall let you know immediately.
Hoping to hear from you soon in regard to what you
have heard from your son, and hoping that it is good
news, I remain, Sincerely yours, Margaret L. Kurtz.[26]*

At Stalag Luft III, my father was always looking for ways to fill
the endless hours. He spent the majority of his day reading in his
barracks. The fact that he rarely ventured outside made him a valuable commodity to the men organizing the digging of escape tunnels.
He was asked to be a lookout for the tunnelers, alerting them to
the whereabouts of "ferrets," the prisoners' name for the German
guards whose purpose was to obtain information about possible
escape attempts. Since my father always read by the window that
had a clear view of the compound yard, if tunneling was in progress
and ferrets were seen approaching the barracks area, my dad would
drop his book, his part in a relay of subtle signals that allowed the
prisoners time enough to cover up their tunnel entrance. His con-
tributions to the well-organized warning system gave him a sorely
needed sense of worth and purpose. In addition, he knew if he was
caught spying on the ferrets, his punishment would be a couple of
days in the cooler, whereas the tunnelers, if caught, might be shot.

Life at Stalag Luft III was not ideal, but at Stalag Luft IV, treatment of prisoners and conditions were significantly worse. Stalag
Luft IV was the POW camp where the remaining crew members of
Sugar Baby were imprisoned. It was located northeast of Sagan in
Gross Tychow, Pomerania.[27] The Luftwaffe respected their captives
at Stalag Luft III; the opposite was true at Stalag Luft IV. For the
most part, the guards were overbearing and cruel. Amenities such
as playing fields and libraries were sparse.

In contrast, the prisoners at Stalag Luft III were allowed to build
a theater and they put on a new show almost every week. Musical
instruments were available and the productions were surprisingly
good. Initially, although not a participant, my dad enjoyed them.

The library, athletic fields, and theater provided the prisoners with a much-needed distraction from kriegie life, if only for a few hours a week. But in time, these activities, which raised the spirits of many of the prisoners, often had an opposite and melancholic effect on my father. Too often he would hear a song, read something in a book, or inhale a familiar scent from the surrounding forest that would remind him of home. He wrote to his parents on September 16, 1944:

> *Dearest Folks, Our daily routine goes on much as usual. A little exercise and sunlight, a lot of reading, and the rest bull-sessions and games to pass the time. Since I've been here I've seen a movie and two musical comedies, the latter produced and acted by local talent which is very good. I finish a book about every two days. As I mentioned in my last letter to Peggy, our room is a veritable League of Nations which makes for interest as well as friendly argument. I don't think I've ever mentioned that we were shot down over the Austrian Alps. I've tried to write the story of those first couple of days but somehow it's hard to get the various feelings and impressions into words—I'll tell you about it when I get home. You, Peggy and Bobby are always in my thoughts. I can't wait for the day when all this ends and we're together again. I'll be seeing you all again soon. Love, Bob.*

Autumn arrived and with it, cooler temperatures and shorter days. Joe Spontak visited my father a few times, and while they enjoyed the friendly banter, after a few minutes, my dad found himself without much to say. Spontak was disturbed to see his good friend so depressed; his attempts at humor barely elicited a smile. It was something Joe would never forget. In excerpts from letters my dad wrote to his parents, his mental downswing is obvious as his hopes for a Christmas homecoming wane.

> *It's so hard to know what to write you, it seems that every day is just a duplicate of the one before. The weather's getting cooler now. The big thing each day is the news, we've all planned our homecoming at least a thousand times.* (September 27, 1944)

Having nice fall weather here but would much rath-er be enjoying it with you at home. U S mail is just starting to come through, so my hopes are getting high but it may still be a couple of months till I hear from you. (October 15, 1944)

Wish my letters were more newsy, but now that it's colder I do nothing but eat, sleep, and read so there isn't much to comment on till your letters start to arrive. I think of you an awful lot. (October 29, 1944)

Boredom, lack of mail, and worries about the oncoming winter were taking their toll. Although outwardly pleasant and amiable, my father was beginning to withdraw emotionally. Nonetheless, he was nothing like the British fellow whose mental state had reached the level where he found it hard to get out of bed. Basically, my father was just sad; his heart ached with every thought of home.

In late autumn, he came up with an idea to occupy his time. On November 9, 1944, he wrote to his parents:

Everything here goes on much the same as usual. I've finally devised an idea to fill a lot of my spare time. I've started a weekly Yank newspaper with letters, of course, as our only source of news. We make the rounds of about 500 Yanks each week, compile any news they give us, have it illustrated by a Yank cartoonist on the camp, type it up, and post it on our central bulletin board. It's a lot of work, especially getting it started but it's a fine time-filler. I'm sure looking forward to hearing from you and Peggy, it seems so long since I've had any word from any of you. I imagine your grandson is getting to be quite a big fellow these days. I can't quite picture him walking alone, talking, and growing up so as he must be. I'm still hoping to be with you all for Christmas. Take care of yourselves. I'll be home soon. Lots of love, Bob.

With Thanksgiving and Christmas rapidly approaching, my father and fellow prisoners at Stalag Luft III resigned themselves to the fact that they would be spending the holidays in the last place on earth they wanted to be. The weather changed dramatically. Upper

Silesia was known for its fierce winters. The men, already dealing with hunger and disease, now had the cold as their enemy. Firewood and coal were extremely scarce. The prisoners sewed newspapers into the linings of their clothes for warmth, preparing for a long, miserable winter.

The upcoming holidays were obviously affecting everyone. My father could think of nothing else. Letters dated late fall and early winter of 1944 confirmed his obsession:

> *The first issue of our Yank paper was quite a success and we have the machinery well organized to print a copy each week now. At present, I'm working on a special Thanksgiving church service. I'll let you know how it turns out. Had our first snow this week but so far haven't had very severe weather.* (November 21, 1944)

> *I've spent the last week reading so consequently have nothing very much to add to my last card. I hope you all had a happy Thanksgiving, we're still holding faint hopes for Christmas but I'm afraid it just isn't going to be this year. Still looking forward to my first letter—it'll be a wonderful day!* (November 29, 1944)

> *I imagine you are all very busy about now getting ready for Christmas—it hardly seems that it's only two weeks away. I hope that you'll have as merry a one as possible—I'll be thinking of you all through the day. It's gotten quite cold here but I'm comfortable and well. Thanksgiving service came off fine.* (December 10, 1944)

It was mid-December and the compound grounds were covered with deep snow. Temperatures hovered near zero and the prisoners only ventured outside for roll calls and the latrine. With all the recreational fields covered, there was no place to exercise. Small arguments broke out among bunkmates who were getting tired of looking at each other every waking hour. The barren, snow-covered terrain accentuated an already bleak existence, and my father thought that if it weren't for the barbed wire and guard towers, he could have been looking at Antarctica. Pat Logan had stopped by the week before with a poem he had written down that described the emptiness and entrapment that the prisoners were feeling:

Barbed Wire in the Morning
Barbed Wire at Night
Nothing but Barbed Wire in
Darkness or Light
Stakes Made of Pinewood,
Strands Made of Steel
A Horrible Nightmare—by God but
It's Real
Asleep in the Moonlight, Awake
in the Sun
Nothing but Barbed Wire, Uniform
and a Gun
Captive in Body, Spirit and Mind
Captive by Barbed Wire Twisted
and Twined
Barbed Wire all Shining
Glistening with Wet
Barbed Wire all Rusted – You
Cannot Forget That Barbed Wire
Surrounds by Night and Day
To Stop You Escaping and Getting Away

Courtesy Pat Logan, Jr.

Several thousand miles away, it was the week before Christmas in White Plains, New York. My mother was busy preparing for the holidays; Bobby was excited about a visit from Santa Claus. Decorations were everywhere, and my mom smiled through her tears as she remembered how she and Bob had decorated their little apartment in Casper, Wyoming, just one year before. She missed him terribly. She sat down to write a letter, one he would receive months later; dated December 17, 1944, it read:

My own dearest one, Well darling another week has passed, one that was spent mostly addressing Christmas cards and wrapping out of town presents. Then

*tonight was the White Gift service at church. It was
beautiful, but when I thought of last year and our going to those things together, I came very near to tears.
Somehow, Christmas can't be much without you, sweet.
I miss you more than ever if that is possible. Bobby, I
imagine, will save the day and I only wish you had him
to help yours. Oh, honey, I love you so very much, with
all my heart every minute of the day and night. Bobby
has been doing something this past week that makes me
happier than I've been since you went. Your picture is on
the table at the foot of the stairs, and every night when
he goes up to bed, he leans over to it and says, "bye, Daddy" and quite often kisses the picture. No one told him to,
darling, he just did. I'm sure he remembers you honey
as we both want him to so much. I so often wonder what
you're doing, if you're going to classes, any sports, etc.
Maybe I'll get a letter soon and know. It would mean so
much. Well, honey, once more I'll say good night and
pray that soon I can say it personally in your arms.
Hurry home to Bobby and I, sweet, you're everything to
us. We both send you kisses, wet ones from Bobby and
all gone ones from me. Your very own, Peggy.*

My father didn't receive this letter until February or March of
1945, after he had been evacuated from Stalag Luft III and relocated
to another camp. It's hard to imagine the joy it must have brought
him when he opened it. From the day he got it, the letter never left
his person. He brought it home with him, where it eventually became
another memento in the green box.

On Christmas morning, 1944, my father awoke in his North Compound barracks at Stalag Luft III to an eerie quiet. A few inches of
finely powdered snow had fallen overnight and elicited that wonderful hush that typically follows a snowstorm. It had been years
since he had witnessed a white Christmas and the irony was not
lost on him that it was occurring in the worst possible place on
earth...a POW camp in Sagan, Germany. He could not deny the
beauty of it, but being unable to share it with his family dampened
his spirits considerably. He was looking forward to his Christmas
dinner; each prisoner had been given a special Red Cross holiday
parcel with turkey and some trimmings. Later that afternoon, the

magical sound of sleigh bells was heard, and as he glanced up, my father saw a sleigh with Santa Claus himself aboard, and two kriegies dressed as reindeer pulling it. Inside were numerous canvas bags, but on this particular Christmas they did not contain gifts or toys. It was something infinitely more precious to the prisoners— mail from home. The American commanders of the camp had purposely held back recently arrived mail until Christmas. My dad had not received one letter from home since his arrival there four months previous. Looking at all those mail bags in the sleigh, he was overcome with joy, thinking to himself, "My waiting is finally over, there has to be a letter for me from Peggy or Mom or Dad." He ran up to the sleigh, cutting in front of other anxious prisoners, oblivious to their grumblings. Santa opened the first bag and began calling out

PRISONERS OF WAR BULLETIN

Published by the American National Red Cross for the Relatives of American Prisoners of War and Civilian Internees

VOL. 2, NO. 12   WASHINGTON, D. C.   DECEMBER 1944

The 1944 Christmas Package

Christmas Package No. 2, packed by women volunteers in the Philadelphia Center during the hottest days of the summer, reached Germany via Sweden in time for distribution to American prisoners of war and civilian internees held by Germany.

The ten thousand Christmas packages sent in 1943 for American prisoners of war and civilian internees in Europe were hardly sufficient to go around, although at the time of ordering, the number seemed excessive. No chances were taken this year. The total shipped in September was fully 50 percent in excess of the number of Americans reported held by Germany at that time, and much more than sufficient to cover those captured since September.

Similarly, all preparations were made—insofar as they could be by the International Committee of the Red Cross and the American Red Cross—to get the packages in time to all camps and hospitals in Germany housing American prisoners. They were shipped, along with large quantities of standard food packages and other supplies, on Red Cross vessels from Philadelphia to Goteborg, Sweden, and thence transshipped to cover vessels to a north German port fairly close to the camps where the largest numbers of Americans are now held. The aim, of course, was to avoid railroad transport in Germany as much as possible.

Much thought was given to planning the 1944 package—the basis of it being "turkey and the 'fixins'." A complete list of the contents follows:

Plum pudding .... 1 lb.
Turkey, boned meat .... ¾ lb.
Small sausages .... ¼ lb.
Strawberry jam .... 6 oz.
Candy, assorted .... ¾ lb.
Deviled ham .... 5 oz.
Cheddar cheese .... ¼ lb.
Nuts, mixed .... ¾ lb.
Bouillon cubes 12
Fruit bars 2
Dates .... 14 oz.
Cherries, canned .... 6 oz.
Playing cards .... 1 pack
Chewing gum .... 4 pkgs.
Butter .... 5¾ oz.
Games, assorted .... 1 box
Cigarettes .... 3 pkgs.
Smoking tobacco .... 1 pkg.
Pipe 1
Tea .... 1¾ oz.
Honey .... 6 oz.
Washcloth 1
Pictures (American scenes) 2

The packages were paid for by the United States government, and the contents in large part were purchased through the Department of Agriculture.

Left unsaid, but implicit in every package, were the heartfelt wishes of the American people for the safe and speedy return of their kinsfolk.

Unfortunately, it was not possible to get a special Christmas package to American prisoners held by Japan, but it is to be hoped earnestly that the large shipment of relief supplies held in Vladivostok, which was picked up by the Japanese steamer *Hakusan Maru* early in November, will reach the camps in time for distribution at Christmas, just as the *Gripsholm* supplies reached the men in most of the camps by Christmas.

Contents of the 1944 Christmas package for American prisoners of war and civilian internees in Europe. More than 15,000 of these packages were shipped from Philadelphia.

Red Cross Bulletin with picture of Christmas Package
contents delivered to Stalag Luft III, December 1944

names of the boys lucky enough to have gotten mail. He stood there shivering in the cold, knee-deep snow, desperately needing to hear his name called out. More than once, his hopes were crushed when the name Robert was called, but sadly, not followed by Kurtz. He tired quickly of other kriegies showing off their letters, his jealousy getting the best of him. Hours later, they opened the last bag but he still would not allow himself to give up hope. Finally, the last letter was handed out and he momentarily slumped to the ground, coming to grips with the fact he would have to wait for another day for some word from home. Moments later, he pulled himself together and knew what he had to do. He went back to his barracks and forced himself to write a letter to his parents, one in which he valiantly tried to hide his disappointment:

> *Dearest Folks, Merry Christmas to you all, I hope you are having a happy day together. I'll be thinking of each of you all day and wishing with all my heart that I could be there with you. Last night I went to a carol service in the compound and today to celebrate Christmas we got our special Xmas parcel which contained canned turkey, pudding, candy, etc. It sure was good! The weather here the last ten days has been sub-zero and snowy so we stick pretty close to the fire. How did your grandson enjoy his second Christmas—if he's the same little monkey I'll bet he was into everything. Haven't been doing much reading lately but expect to start again soon. Merry Christmas to you all again, take real good care of yourselves. Lots of love, Bob.*

Conditions at Stalag Luft III continued to deteriorate throughout the month of January. The fierce cold undermined the kriegies' already precarious health. Pneumonia and other serious upper respiratory ailments were a problem for many of the prisoners; outbreaks of disease were a huge concern. There was little medication, if any, to treat the men and many of them were contagious. Red Cross parcel deliveries were few and far between and even the rationing of black bread had been cut. The men needed nutrition to fight off disease; depletions in the food supply did not bode well for the coming months.

On January 10, 1945, my dad wrote to his folks:

Mail has definitely slackened up with the holidays so I'm still looking forward to my first news from home. Winter has really set in here with snow continually on the ground and most days quite cold. I would appreciate Camels and chocolate in any parcels the Red Cross will let you send. Lots of love, Bob.

My father had been at Stalag Luft III for five months and not received any mail from his wife or parents. In his letter written on Christmas day, he mentioned that although he planned to start again soon, he hadn't done much reading. Reading is what had kept him going through all those months of ennui. He tried to put up a good front in his letters home, but they betray a steady decline in his psyche as the months dragged on. The only thing keeping him alive was his determination to return to his loved ones.

It was late January and exciting news was filtering in to the prisoners from handmade radios they had secretly hidden in their barracks. The Russian Army had mobilized a huge offensive of millions of soldiers and was steamrolling across Poland, their sights on Berlin and beyond. George Patton and his Third Army were much further away but were methodically driving eastward. Rumors of liberation by the Russians were circulating in the compound; the men finally had something to hope for. Conversely, they feared that Hitler would have them all shot. According to some Allied radio reports, he had ordered the deaths of millions of Jews. What difference would it make to dispose of a few thousand more prisoners of war? Hitler feared that if the Russians arrived first at the prison camps, the liberated POWs would join forces with them. The Führer eventually agreed not to take the prisoners lives. Instead, he ordered an immediate evacuation of the camps, Stalag Luft III included.

January 27, 1945 began as every other day had, except for one very notable thing: artillery fire echoed through the valleys of Upper Silesia, and it was close by. It woke the men, who began excitedly talking among themselves. The men who had trained in artillery school in the States estimated that the Russians were as close as 20 kilometers. They noticed that the guards were also visibly affected by the proximity of the shelling, yet roll call went on as usual and the men returned to their barracks. Despite everyone being on edge, they stuck to their regular schedules. There was a hockey game in one compound and a musical production in another. After 10:00 p.m. roll call, the prisoners lingered a little bit longer outside their barracks; everyone wanted to know what the hell was going on.

My father went to bed early. Like the other men, his hopes of liberation had been dashed, at least for that day. Snow was falling and the temperature had dropped below zero. He tossed and turned, frustrated that he couldn't get warm. Finally, he slept. A huge commotion awakened him. He looked at his watch. It was 11:00 p.m. and the guards were screaming "Raus! Raus!" He looked outside to see thousands of prisoners assembling in the compound. They were being ordered to evacuate the camp and were given only a few hours to gather up all their belongings. The wind was howling and there was close to a foot of snow on the ground. Everyone wondered not only where they were going, but also how in God's name they would be able to transport their food and clothing through the ever-deepening snow. They were told that each prisoner would get their own Red Cross parcel. This was both welcome and troubling news. They were glad to have the extra food supply, but realized it would add more than ten pounds to the already heavy loads they had put together. With only a couple of hours to figure out the best method to carry their belongings, some of the men came up with ingenious solutions.

A few of the prisoners fashioned sleds by using bunk bed slats as runners for the snow and nailing them to boards they had ripped up from the barracks floors. Some men still had their Red Cross cardboard suitcases from Dulag Luft and they threaded ropes through the handles, tied them around their waists, and dragged them through the snow. Most of these lasted only a couple of days; once soaking wet, they shredded and were useless. Many of the POWs made backpacks out of blankets, only to find out a few hours into the evacuation that the melting snow had doubled them in weight, too heavy to manage.

In the late hours of January 27 and the early morning of January 28, 1945, approximately 11,000 kriegies began the evacuation of Stalag Luft III as snow began to fall.[28] One of them was my father. He felt exhilarated as he passed through the gates that had slammed shut on him five months previously. He knew that if he could endure the elements, he would no longer be *gefangenen-nummer* 7241.

My father still had not received any mail from home. He would have to endure the harshest experience of his life before he would receive his first letter. He tucked little Bobby's slipper securely in the inside pocket of his jacket, hoping to keep it safe and dry. Head down into the driving snow, he joined the endless line of prisoners that stretched for miles.

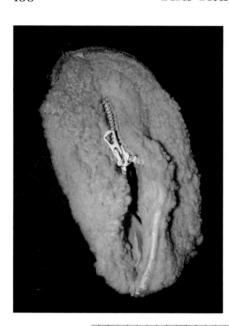

THIS PAGE

top
Bobby's baby slipper

bottom
Stalag Luft III identification form for
2nd Lt. Robert R. Kurtz, August 1944

FACING PAGE

top
Jim with Hilde Richter,
Hotel Tirolerhof reception,
August 3, 2001

bottom
From left to right:
Elley Leitner, Jim Kurtz, Gerd
Leitner, Mike Kurtz, Connie Beson,
Col. and Mrs. Bruce Boevers, Debbie
Beson, Tim Beson, Willi Unger,
August 3, 2001

ABOVE

Memorial cross on the Brendlkar, August 4, 2001

FACING PAGE

top
Reconciled adversaries at Ehrwald Commemoration, August 3, 2001
Joe Spontak in center flanked by Oskar Bösch on his right and Willi Unger on his left

bottom
Memorial in the village square, Ehrwald, Austria, dedicated on August 3, 2001
to the Americans and Germans killed in action on August 3, 1944

THIS PAGE

top
Hilde Richter, her
brother, and mother on
the Ehrwalder Alm,
August 3, 1944
Courtesy Hilde Richter

bottom
Julie and Jim Kurtz
on the same rock
exactly 66 years later

FACING PAGE

top
Revisiting the Brendklar,
August 3, 2010.
From left: Gerd Leitner,
Julie and Jim

bottom
Jim holding a piece of
Sugar Baby's wing found
over 1,000 meters from
the Brendlkar crash
site, August 3, 2010

FACING PAGE

top
Meeting Tony Jezowski,
Linwood, Michigan,
Summer 2006

bottom
Jim with George
Britton, Boca Raton,
Florida, June 2011

THIS PAGE

top:
Returning Charlie
Sellars' wedding
ring to his brother
Ken, Fall 2010

bottom:
Jim in the co-pilot seat
of a B-24 Liberator at
the Collings Foundation
Air Show, Summer 2013

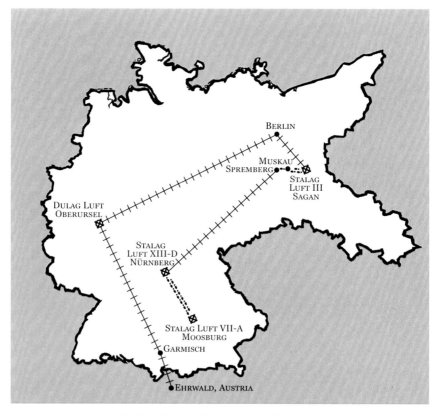

My father's route from capture to liberation

8/3/44:	Shot down in Ehrwald, Austria
8/3/44:	Ehrwald to Garmisch, 13 miles
8/7–8/10/44:	Garmisch to Oberursel, 212 miles
8/13/–8/15/44:	Oberursel to Berlin, 392 miles
8/15–8/16/44:	Berlin to Sagan, 100 miles
1/29/45:	Stalag Luft III evacuated
1/29–1/31/45:	Sagan to Muskau, 35 miles
2/1/45:	Muskau to Spremberg, 16 miles
2/2–2/4/45:	Spremberg to Nürnberg, 251 miles
4/4–4/14/45:	Nürnberg to Moosburg, 94 miles
4/29/45:	Liberated

THE MARCH HOME

There can be no doubt that the ten thousand or more despairing men of Luft III who 'hit the road' that momentous night as hope sounded from the east, will ever remember the tortuous trek that followed in the ever-increasing fury of the blizzard. Snow fell for four days in near-zero temperatures. Ill-fitting packs, blisters, frozen feet and hands, and sickness all contributed to the misery of the marchers groping their way to some undisclosed destination beyond the reach of encroaching Russian armies.[1]

—Bob Neary, "Stalag Luft III"

THE THOUSANDS OF KRIEGIES EVACUATED FROM STALAG Luft III on January 27-28, 1945, formed a line that, according to historians, snaked and twisted its way through the deep snow for more than 20 miles. Weary and half-frozen from being forced out of their barracks, the prisoners set out on an epic journey later dubbed "The Forced March." The British RAF officers called it "The Long March." Some even went as far as labeling it "The Death March." Regardless of the title, all agreed it was a nightmare.

Two thousand men from South Compound were the first to be ordered out of the camp. It was their unenviable task to act as a human plow, walking in rows four men wide, tamping down the six inches of snow that had already fallen on the roads out of Sagan. Their position was far worse than that of the 9,000 men who followed. Within minutes, their clothing was drenched. The physical strain of shuffling through the still-falling snow had them sweating profusely, and the frigid temperatures caused the men's perspiration to freeze on their bodies. It had proven to be a curse to be selected as the first men evacuated: the prisoners of South Compound would suffer with debilitating frostbite much sooner and with greater magnitude than the prisoners that followed literally in their footsteps.

The West Compound was next to evacuate Stalag Luft III, at approximately 1:00 a.m., January 28. My father and the rest of North Compound left at 4:00 a.m.; the Center Compound followed immediately afterward. Finally, at 6:00 a.m., the East Compound fell into line. Amazingly, close to 11,000 Allied prisoners were evacuated in less than eight hours.[2] The Germans had thousands of Red Cross parcels in storage. Excluding the South Compound, each kriege was issued one for the evacuation march. Even so, over 23,000 remained in storage facilities. Cigarettes were a well-known bartering tool and many of the prisoners had accumulated several cartons for that purpose. Scrambling to prepare for evacuation, they grabbed as many as they could, stuffing them into their pockets or loading them on sledges. Between the Red Cross parcels hoarded by the Germans and cartons of cigarettes the kriegies were unable to carry, it is estimated that the total number of cigarettes left behind at Stalag Luft III was a staggering 4,000,000![3]

As the last of the East Compound exited the gates and went out into the cold and unpredictable night, fires erupted within the camp. A wry smile of satisfaction formed on my dad's lips as he watched the barracks in North Compound that had been his home from hell for five months begin to burn. The blazing camp lit up the night sky as my father and the rest of the prisoners slowly marched away.

Within hours, the morale that had been so high the night before was beginning to spiral downward. Although finally free from the confines of Stalag Luft III, myriad problems challenged the men's hopes for eventual freedom. The snow continued to fall, footing was treacherous, and fierce winds penetrated the marchers' saturated clothing. Every new gust felt like a freezing dagger, chilling each man to the bone. Unaware of the length of the upcoming journey, many were unwilling to carry the extra pounds of food that had been issued in the Red Cross parcels the night before and wolfed down their contents. Marching with a full belly proved to be catastrophic; many of the men vomited, their shrunken stomachs unable to accommodate the large meal.

My father and fellow kriegies were grateful for the light of dawn. Daybreak revealed a sight that none of them would ever forget: shivering men, hunched over, trudging at a snail's pace through knee-deep snow, forming a line of human misery that stretched to the horizon both behind and in front of them as far as the eye could see.

Although the guards kept the lines moving, they were not overly harsh in their treatment of the prisoners since they were in the same boat as their captives. Remarkably, there were some kriegies who were in better shape than the guards, who were for the most part older, overweight men, or young soldiers still recovering from combat wounds.[4] The weather conditions and lack of adequate food affected friend and foe alike. Friendships had been formed between the guards and the kriegies at Stalag Luft III, a fact that became increasingly clear as the days of the march progressed. Weary and incapacitated guards were lifted onto horse-pulled wagons by prisoners, thus saving their lives. George Britton recalled, "One of the goons ordered me to carry his rifle. He was an older, overweight man and it was just too heavy for him to carry any more. To this day, I don't know if it was loaded or not."

The coldest winter in 50 years showed no signs of letting up as my father and his fellow bunkmates huddled together for body warmth. Even though the Germans allowed for short rest periods each day, some of the men were showing signs of frostbite and they needed respite from the elements. Nightfall approached and questions arose as to where the prisoners would camp. The answer was Muskau, a small industrial city approximately 35 miles from Sagan.

POWs pulling makeshift sleds through the snow on the Long March
Courtesy USAFA McDermott Library MS 329

Kriegies huddle together for warmth during a rare rest stop on the Long March
Courtesy USAFA McDermott Library MS 329

What must the prisoners have felt as they approached the town of Muskau? The fierce Silesian winter and nearly 48-hour march had brought them to their knees. Muskau was not a large city and they wondered how it could possibly accommodate the thousands of kriegies who poured into its midst. Even if they were fortunate enough to find a building with a roof still intact, there were no guarantees that war-weary locals wouldn't kill them as they slept.

Britton remembers a harrowing moment, being marched towards a brick factory for escape from the fierce cold. Although desperate for protection from the elements, he and many of the prisoners hesitated to go inside. Two tall smokestacks rose above the main factory building. Reports had been filtering in about concentration camps and the atrocities committed there. George said that no one knew they were entering a glass factory; they thought they were being led to the ovens.

Other prisoners, close to 2,000 and mostly from Center Compound, took refuge in a small church that normally would have held 200 worshippers.[5] Perhaps my father was among them. There was not one inch to spare; they lay down next to each other, elbow to elbow, making it impossible to even roll over. Some were so exhausted they were unable to stand to relieve themselves and unashamedly urinated where they slept. The rigors of the march had intensified the men's relentless hunger. For every group of 20 prisoners, the Germans issued one loaf of black bread accompanied by a slab of ersatz margarine that could cause a nasty bout of diarrhea within hours. The latrines were few and far between. Everywhere in the city, whether church, factory, or barn, the prisoners were forced to lie in their own urine and feces. Those fortunate enough to have found shelter in the church would have witnessed what fellow prisoner Kenneth W. Simmons described in his book entitled *Kriegie: Prisoner of War*:

> The church was packed so that any man who found it necessary to move more than a few feet was almost certain to step on someone else ... Toilets were set up outside, and there was a continuous line to and from them. With two thousand men in one small building, lines were moving all night long. Many men became desperately sick at their stomachs and were never able to reach the door. Dozens of men rushed up aisles vomiting all the way. Others with dysentery stepped on hands, feet, and stomachs, trying to get outside. Nerves were strained to the breaking point.[6]

In addition to the church, every factory in the industrial city was filled to capacity with kriegies. The men knew that German factories were primary targets for Allied bombers, but they were just too tired to care. Thousands of prisoners spent two nights in Muskau, partly because the guards were as worn out as their captives. On the morning of February 1, 1945, they resumed their march. Their destination was Spremberg, Germany.

An unexpected thaw the day before had turned the road into a quagmire. Within minutes, the prisoners' boots were soaked with water and mud. It made for slow going as the men stopped constantly to retrieve a shoe they had stepped out of in the unyielding muck. To compound the situation, the temperature was falling and it began to snow again. It was 16 miles to Spremberg, and it would take almost all day. My father and the rest of the 11,000 men in the lines grew more miserable by the hour. The water in their boots froze; aching numbness defined every footstep, and they willed themselves to keep moving to prevent loss of circulation. Hunger and thirst were constant companions. Most of the men had already exhausted their allotment of food from the Red Cross, and some of the marchers were so weak they abandoned whatever remained of the heavy parcels on the side of the road, unable to bear their weight any longer. The kriegies from Center and East Compounds brought up the rear of the over 20-mile-long stretch of men and therefore benefitted by scavenging through discarded food for any scraps that might have been left behind.

The prisoners from Stalag Luft III were not alone on the highways and roads that led south from Sagan. The Russian Army was steamrolling through Eastern Europe, determined to avenge atrocities committed earlier in the war when the Germans had invaded their homeland. Now they were exceedingly close, having driven through Poland and the northeast border of Germany. The farther south the kriegies marched, the more refugees they encountered. Terror-stricken Polish and German citizens had gathered up whatever belongings they could and set out on the highways in record numbers. Lt. Richard Schiefelbusch, who had been a prisoner at Stalag Luft III for more than two years, wrote:

> One of the principal aspects of our march was the excessive number of civilians, especially old people and children who were crowding the roads as we moved to our still unknown destination. They were, of course, trying to escape to avoid the Russian armies that were overrunning their villages and their homes. The estimates that were given in the historical account of this migration was 6,000,000 people. They were mainly Polish and German. It was the most abject, massive human tragedy that I have ever seen. The procession included people with small horse drawn carts, wagons, and people with sleds and people with backpacks, all trying to survive.[7]

The road from Muskau to Spremberg was now a river of refugees. With the influx of the fleeing civilians, enterprising prisoners bartered with them for some of their belongings. A hundred American cigarettes was enough to purchase a cart or wagon that they would fill with Red Cross parcels and anything else to lighten the marchers' load. Some traded specifically for food; an egg or a loaf of bread were treasured items. Thoughts of the millions of cigarettes left behind at Stalag Luft III and the food for which they could have been traded tormented more than a few of the men.

Surviving the initial days of the march and driven by the desire to make it home to Peggy and Bobby, my father arrived in Spremberg on the night of February 1, 1945. Cold, hungry, and frightened, he again found shelter for the night.

The guards roused the prisoners the next morning and marched them to the railway yards. Although a few were passenger cars for German citizens, most railway cars were the dreaded "40 and 8s" built by the French to accommodate forty men and eight horses during World War I.[8] My dad saw they were eerily similar to the rail cars that had been jammed with black-and-white clad men and women a few months ago in Garmisch. He had wondered then about the cruelty and inhumanity associated with those overcrowded cars; he was now about to find out for himself.

The night before, they had been issued a tiny portion of black bread along with some ersatz margarine and a small portion of hot barley soup. With no idea how long they would be without facilities, the men were forced to squat in the freshly fallen snow as diarrhea ravaged their intestines. Dehydration was of great concern to the prisoners and the lack of drinking water was becoming a huge problem. Although he was referring to a different German town named Regensburg, Simmons recounts the necessity for water in *Kriegie: Prisoner of War*:

> All of us started hollering, '*Wasser, Wasser.*' We had made up our minds that we were either going to get some water or die. The station was crowded with civilians trying to board trains. There was a pond just ahead of the engine, and there were water fountains in the station. We broke ranks en masse, and started for the pond and water fountains. Guards fired in the air, but all of us moved to the water. Men drank and filled their cans and jars with water.

> Until that moment, I had never realized the value of plain water...It was the most valuable necessity of life, without water men became animals.[9]

After drinking whatever water they were lucky enough to find, the prisoners were led to each of the 40 and 8s. Most had exhausted their allotments of supplies from the Red Cross parcels. They were forced to leave behind what little food they had. The already starving men were left with nothing to eat at all.

Sixty prisoners and two guards were assigned to each 40 and 8. Crammed together, they were unable to sit or lie down. For most that was just fine because the floors were ankle-deep in both human and animal excrement. The prisoners hadn't bathed in weeks. In the overloaded cars, the stench was overwhelming, causing many of the men to vomit. After a few hours, it became obvious that the guards were not going to stop the trains for the men to relieve themselves. Eventually, nature ran its course and the men were left with no choice. Although each car had a waste bucket in its corner, it filled quickly. Urine, human waste, and vomit accumulated on the rail car floors at an alarming rate. The men endured these conditions for three days. They were without water for more than 36 hours. On the second day, the cars ground to a halt and the prisoners were allowed to exit the train for a few minutes. My father's bombardier, George Britton, described the scene: "As the cattle car doors slid open, we literally trampled each other in our frenzy to get out. All you could see from one end of the fields to the other was a line of men with pants down around their ankles. That damned lard was the problem, we were so hungry that we ate it and paid the price every time. To see all those bare asses as we shit out in those fields was like looking at one long line of moons. It's funny now, but I'll promise you, it wasn't funny at all when it happened."

The prisoners tried to care for the men who were acutely ill. They cleared the floors as best they could so that the sick could lie down; the result was that healthier men sometimes had to sleep on top of each other. Their concern for the ailing kriegies was commendable, but there were less commendable actions too, with reports of a few captains and colonels pulling rank and ordering their men to clear the floors, so that they could lay down themselves in more comfort.

At the end of the second day, both prisoners and guards alike were becoming severely dehydrated. The kriegies, under German guard supervision, searched desperately for water. When they returned to the train, the prisoners lingered as long as they could. No one wanted to get back inside those cars; the stench emanating from the open doors was overpowering and the only ventilation was two open slats on the roof of the car. The two guards inside each car eventually took turns being outside, with one standing on the roof of the car to escape the filth while the other suffered the same plight as the kriegies.

Finally, on February 4, the cattle cars laden with exhausted and sick POWs pulled into the city of Nürnberg. The men poured out of the train and drew huge gulps of fresh air. This time it was the locals who were treated to the sight of hundreds of squatting men; there had been only two rest stops in three days. For the prisoners, it was exquisite just to be able to stretch their limbs outside of the confines of the 40 and 8s. Most of the men hadn't eaten or drunk anything for 72 hours, and obtaining water was their first priority. Swarms of the parched POWs surged to the holding tanks of water used for the steam engines of the locomotives. They were warned about contamination but were unable to resist gulping down the tainted liquid. It was utter chaos as the search for water continued. Guards were as thirsty as the kriegies and knocked them down as they rushed to the local drinking fountain, leaving their prisoners unattended. Eventually, some semblance of order was restored and the men were ordered into groups. Shortly thereafter, they were marched at gunpoint to Stalag XIII-D on the outskirts of Nürnberg. A few days earlier, the Germans had ordered Italian POWs evacuated from the camp in order to make room for the incoming kriegies from Sprem- berg. This vermin-infested, disease-filled camp was to be my father's home for the next two months.

The Long March had been horrible, and the three days of hell in the livestock cars even worse, but nothing could have prepared my father for conditions at Stalag XIII-D. Everyone was initially grateful to get a break from the grueling battle against the elements that had defined the Long March. It took them less than a day to discover they might have been better off to still be on the road.

Ravenous upon their arrival at the camp, they had anticipated new Red Cross parcels, but there were none. German rations were paltry to say the least. Three hundred grams of black bread, two hundred-fifty grams of potatoes, and a small slab of margarine made up the kriegies' diet.[10] A new soup was introduced at Stalag XIII-D. Unlike the "nutritious" green death soup at Stalag Luft III, flour and water were the sole ingredients in what the prisoners aptly labeled the "gray death soup." It was a constant source of intestinal distress and, like every other part of their meager diet, sent the men running to the latrines regularly. The starving men were losing weight at an alarming rate, and as the weeks went by, more prisoners arrived and food was even harder to come by.

Lack of food was only one of the many challenges the kriegies encountered in Nürnberg. Sleeping conditions in the filthy barracks were deplorable. Because the exteriors of the buildings were in terrible shape, holes in the roofs and missing boards from the walls allowed lice, bedbugs, and fleas to infiltrate the living quarters. With no insecticides or powders to discourage them, they crawled unchecked in the men's bedding and clothing. Prisoners awakened to discover scores of insect bites on every exposed part of their bodies. Rats were everywhere and as the men dozed off to sleep at night, thoughts of rodents chewing on their ears and faces led to nightmares that jarred them awake. Lying there shivering and drenched in sweat, they found themselves unable to fall back to sleep.

The hideous conditions my father and the kriegies lived with every day drained them mentally as well as physically. The futility of their situation made the men question how much more could they take and, more importantly, whether they would survive their ordeal. Stalag XIII-D was located on the outskirts of Nürnberg, which was being bombed by the Allies day and night. The prisoners' nerves were raw and the sound of sirens warning of impending attacks by the bombers sent the men scurrying to slit trenches or whatever cover they could find. The Allies were aware of the POW camp's location and did their best to avoid it, but there was always a chance that strong winds or poor weather could cause their bombs to fall unpredictably. The night raids were the worst. Mind-staggering light shows lit up the prison campgrounds as flares used by the Allies to illuminate the city of Nürnberg for more precision bombing turned night into day. The concussion from the ordinance exploding nearby shook the ground as well as the men's nerves. For the two months my father remained in the hellhole that was Stalag XIII-D, Nürnberg was bombed nearly every day.

Two and a half weeks passed before my dad was able to obtain the specific stationery required to write home. It would be the last letter that would make it back to the States and eventually into the green box, although he probably wrote many more. In a letter to his parents on February 22, 1945, he attempted to downplay his situation:

> *Dearest Folks, it was wonderful to get Mum's Dec. 3 letter, the only mail I've received so far. Since then we've been moved to another camp and I've been without writing facilities for quite a while. It was such a relief to know that you were all all right. Conditions here aren't quite as good as before but we're making out O.K. Don't worry. Lots of love, Bob.*

He failed to describe the relentless Allied bombing that had occurred two days before he wrote, or that the entire camp had lost all electricity due to the proximity of the air strikes, making a dismal existence even more trying. He did not talk about the fact that daily food rationing was cut down to two pieces of black bread and a half bowl of gray death soup. Nor did he tell his family that it was Nürnberg's coldest winter in 50 years, or that the Germans had decreased the amount of pressed coal used to heat the kriegies' barracks. Food and fuel were scarce for both sides and with the end of the war rapidly approaching, the guards' living conditions were on a par with their captives. Basically, everyone was miserable.

In early March 1945, the prisoners were allowed their first hot shower since leaving Sagan.[11] Although he was only given five minutes to shower, my father was ecstatic for the chance to scrub off six weeks of accumulated filth. The down side was that the men only had one set of clothes. Therefore, after washing them as best they could, they were left with the dilemma of trying to dry them in winter conditions. More often than not, they had no choice but to put them back on, cold and still wet. Three weeks later, they were again offered showers; this time, however, there was no hot water available and thoughts of showering in sub-freezing conditions discouraged most of the kriegies from accepting the privilege.

By the middle of March, the situation at Stalag XIII-D had deteriorated even more. The lack of fuel for cooking or heating the barracks caused the prisoners to take drastic measures. Standard bunk beds consisted of ten wooden slats that supported the straw-filled mattresses. They now had only three or four; the missing ones were burned for fuel. For those fortunate enough to have a bunk bed, back ailments were common. Many were forced to sleep on frozen mud floors. Parts of the walls were also torn down and added to the fires. Occasionally, a partial thaw in temperature increased the number of vermin, which found the prisoners' mattresses ideal breeding grounds. The incessant bombing of Nürnberg weakened the foundations of the barracks, creating yet more cracks and holes for rats to slither through. All food had to be stored in the kitchen area and anyone foolish enough to attempt to bring food to bed with them could be awakened in the middle of the night by the rodents gnawing their way through their blankets in search of a piece of black bread. The rats didn't always win; the men's hunger was so acute that if they were fortunate to trap one, it might end up as their dinner that evening—cooked or not.

On March 14, 1945, in the midst of unrelenting hardship, Christmas finally arrived at Stalag XIII-D. Three trucks, loaded with Red Cross boxes, rolled into camp.[12] The prisoners could not believe their eyes! Thousands of kriegies were imprisoned at Stalag XIII-D, and the allotment per prisoner was less than a full parcel. Nonetheless, morale skyrocketed among the captives, and smiles were seen on their faces for the first time in weeks. At last there was something to substitute for that damn black bread, whether it was pudding or a piece of cheese. But there was something in those Red Cross boxes that the kriegies craved even more. Cigarettes, oh, those beloved cigarettes! I can picture my dad leaning against the walls of his dilapidated barracks, lighting up a Lucky, inhaling and cherishing that little stick more than anything in the world at that particular moment.

For the most part, the last two weeks of March mirrored the first two. Partial Red Cross shipments continued to make their way through enemy territory, providing the men with much-needed nourishment. Most of the prisoners had lost 30 to 50 pounds, and dysentery, diphtheria, and pneumonia were rampant. But things were looking up. News broadcasts from radios secreted out of Stalag Luft III brought encouraging information about momentous Allied victories as British and American troops surged eastward towards Germany. They had repulsed the Germans in the epic Battle of the Bulge and their sights were now on Berlin and the annihilation of Hitler. Allied superiority was also evident in the skies above the prison camp. P-51 and P-38 American fighters buzzed freely overhead, with no sight of Me-109 and Fw-190 fighters to engage them in dogfights. The American fighters would playfully dip their wings as they passed over the camp, acknowledging their fellow airmen imprisoned below. The Allied bombing raids, while frightening for the kriegies, were an affirmation of their dominance of the skies over Germany. Numerous flak emplacements around Nürnberg had been sabotaged by the Underground, reducing the amount of deadly black puffs exploding amidst the bombers as they rained hell down on the city. By March of 1945, the British and American firepower in the air was clearly superior to that of the Luftwaffe. The kriegies listened daily to radio broadcasts telling of Allied advances, and their hopes grew. But before those hopes were realized, my father and his companions would have to withstand yet another set of challenges.

Aware of the Allied advance from the west as well as the Russian Army's push southward, the German command decided to evacuate Stalag XIII-D on April 3.[13] Unlike at Stalag Luft III, the prisoners were given a day's notice to gather up their belongings for the next stage of the Forced March. The men had mixed emotions. News of the rapidly approaching Third Army led by General George Patton and the possibility of liberation encouraged the prisoners, but that hope was crushed when they were ordered to evacuate Nürnberg. On a brighter note, the fierce winter was thankfully coming to an end. Two days before their departure, a Red Cross shipment of American insecticide had unexpectedly arrived and was already working wonders killing the bloodsucking vermin that had infested the men. Conditions were noticeably better as they prepared to evacuate, but they all agreed on one thing: they could not get out of Nürnberg and the disease-filled camp that was Stalag XIII-D fast enough.

At approximately 10:00 a.m. on April 4, my father fell in line with thousands of other prisoners as they marched out of the nightmare that had been their home for two torturous months. They carried what they could manage, but most had learned not to weigh themselves down with unnecessary items. My father once again tucked the baby slipper inside his clothing and took as many cigarettes as he could. The prisoners had no idea where they were going, or how long it would take to get there. Their destination was Stalag VII-A in Moosburg, Germany, 90 miles distant, and the trip would take ten grueling days.

From the first day out, certain stipulations were agreed upon between the prisoners and the guards. Physically, neither side had much left in their tanks. There had been no place to exercise in the Nürnberg camp and the men were in no shape to march for days. The two sides agreed to have ten-minute rest periods every hour. The guards also allowed the men to stray from the lines in search of food on the condition that they shared whatever they could scrounge up. Adding to their persistent enemies of thirst, hunger, and illness, the kriegies now faced a new and more immediate threat—friendly fire. Reports had come from the rear of the lines that American P-47 Thunderbolt fighter pilots had mistaken the marching prisoners for retreating German troops and had strafed their lines, killing and injuring several POWs.[14]

As had been the case in the march from Sagan to Nürnberg, the guards were becoming more and more dependent on their captives for survival. They knew the war would soon be over and that they were going to lose. They feared repercussions from the prisoners upon their liberation, so any harsh treatment was stopped. They purposely looked away as groups of the prisoners wandered off into the fields or underbrush to escape. There were very few instances of gunfire being used to keep the men in line. Not everyone made it to Stalag VII-A, but the majority did, and all agreed it was a combined effort that saved them—that, and the basic human instinct to survive.

Of all my father's wartime experiences, the ten-day march to Moosburg is the one I know the least about. Interviews with two of his crew members on *Sugar Baby*, George Britton and Joe Spontak, have helped me immensely to understand the desperation they experienced as they hiked, but they had been separated from my dad at Stalag Luft III. Therefore, I can only guess where my father sought shelter for nine nights on his way to Moosburg. Prisoners spent each night wherever they could find an escape from the elements: barns, churches, factories, mills, and even some German houses. The kriegies were constantly in search of food and water. It wasn't uncommon to see American and British airmen on their hands and knees digging for potatoes in the German farm fields. George Britton recalled trading several packs of cigarettes with a local farmer for a few fresh eggs and a piece of cheese. Although a few Red Cross trucks had made it through to the line of men, the little food they brought had been divided up among thousands. Stories were told of kriegies, who had been bunkmates for years, fighting each other over a rotten potato in a pig trough. Towards the end of the ten days, hunger-driven men could be seen on their rest breaks eating the grass they lay on. Heavy rains fell for a couple of days and while it made the footing poor and increased the weight of the men's clothing, it was gratefully received as the men gulped it down and filled whatever containers they could to quench their insatiable thirst. Finally, on April 14, when they were wondering just how much more they could take, my father and his fellow prisoners arrived at Stalag VII-A, Moosburg, Germany. Andrew Turner's account, "The Death March of the Kriegies," defines the camaraderie of the men on the Forced March and his pride and admiration for how they all held together to survive.

> Many of the Kriegies in Stalag Luft III were airmen who had been shot down. They may not have fought the war on the front lines, but they fought a different type of war—a war in their mind. A war against discouragement, hopelessness, and despair was their fight. They battled to keep their fellow Kriegies in high spirits, to make sure they all saw their homes again. A bond developed, a bond allowing them to make the march from Sagan. A union enabling a man to carry a stranger on his back for days through the snow, and to never meet him again was not uncommon. There was an inner strength, empowering a sick man on the verge of death to march through arctic conditions with only a vision of home to move his tired legs. Many of these men never completed the march to Moosburg. However, many more did make it home to their families, careers, and lives.[15]

As the massive gates of Stalag VII-A began to swing open, my father felt a sense of impending doom. It was his third prison camp in nine months and he was unsure of what to expect, but nothing could have prepared him for what his eyes beheld inside the huge confines of the prison yard on the morning of April 14. Hundreds of kriegies from the Forced March were herded into the camp at Moosburg daily. Originally built to house 20,000 prisoners when filled to capacity, it now held more than 130,000.[16] As he looked out at the sea of suffering humanity in front of him, my father was concerned not only about getting enough food, but also about finding shelter for a much needed rest. Barracks that had been constructed to accommodate 200 men held 500, and that was only if one was lucky enough to secure a spot indoors. Thousands of kriegies slept on the ground under huge tents. It was early spring and the combination of melting snow and constant rain showers transformed the surface into a sea of mud. The men had no choice but to lay down in several inches of it to sleep.

The warmer weather reintroduced the vermin nightmare and the majority of the prisoners were forced to deal with the itching and health problems attributed to the pests. Many men were suffering from curable ailments, but with no medications with which to treat them, their conditions grew progressively worse.

The lack of food and water that had plagued the kriegies for months became a matter of much greater concern in Moosburg. Although there were water pumps at Moosburg, they were few and far between, and the prisoners had to rely heavily on rainstorms for drinking water and for cooking. Stalag Luft VII-A was the supply center for Red Cross parcels in southern Germany, and the Germans did their best to see to it that each kriegie would receive one each week, but the sheer number of men imprisoned at Moosburg made that impossible.[17] Even though they found their own strength fading, the healthier men shared their food with those less fortunate.

My father had been at Stalag VII-A only a few hours when word spread among the new arrivals that President Franklin Roosevelt had died two days earlier. Morale, already low, fell to new depths and many of the men wept unashamedly. Others wondered how his death would affect the course of the war. Americans at home, as well as men and women serving abroad, had depended on his fierce and unfaltering leadership. His successor, Harry Truman, was an unknown, and the men feared that having a new executive in office might, in some way, lengthen the war. As POWs thousands of miles away in southern Germany, they were helpless to do anything. Their primary goal was to somehow stay alive for just a few more days and hope for a swift and victorious conclusion to the war.

Each day at Stalag VII-A seemed to blend in with the one before and the one that followed. It had come down to a nerve-wracking waiting game. Reports of Patton's Third Army's advancement through Germany were heard daily on the prisoners' radios, and it gave them hope. The guards were on edge all the time, a promising sign that they, too, knew their war was almost over. Huge formations of Allied heavy bombers were seen daily as they passed over Moosburg, en route to Munich. Low-flying German fighters were spotted over the camp as they tried to avoid confrontations with them. For the first time in months, my father and 130,000 POWs truly believed that their liberation was imminent.

The next day, April 28, dragged on endlessly. Artillery and small-arms fire could be heard around the perimeters of the camp, although there was no visual evidence of American tanks or personnel. As sundown approached, the prisoners went about their evening ritual of cooking what little food they had. After dinner, the weary men laid down and tried to go to sleep. A few hours later, they were awakened by the sound of truck engines and German voices. They rushed from their barracks and out from under their tents to investigate the commotion and came upon a sight they would never forget. The engines they had heard were those of German troop transport trucks and the voices were from the guards as they scrambled into the backs of the vehicles. The majority were escaping into the night, leaving only a skeleton crew behind. There would be no more sleep for the kriegies. Filled with anticipation of the following day's events, they talked among themselves, played games, or took walks to ease the tension.

At daybreak on April 29, the wait was over. It was a Sunday morning and my father and many of the prisoners were preparing to go to church service. American tanks and soldiers of the 14th Armored Division of Patton's Third Army appeared on a hill not far from the front gate of Stalag VII-A. The men looked on anxiously as they began to close in. Suddenly, all hell broke loose. Small-arms fire crackled from every direction. A few German guards and some SS troops who had been fighting the Americans in the streets of Moosburg decided not to surrender; the fight was on. A couple of P-51 American fighters dove from the skies and strafed the guard towers, sending the prisoners scurrying for cover. Bullets whizzed everywhere within the compound as the prisoners hit the ground and crawled into the nearest slit trenches. With freedom only minutes away and having survived months of captivity, sickness, and starvation, they did not want to be casualties of friendly fire.

By early afternoon, all German resistance had been quashed. The prisoners rose from the mud and out of the slit trenches and looked toward the gate at the northern perimeter of the camp. The most beautiful sight in the world met their eyes as a Sherman tank steamrolled through the stockade fence and hated barbed wire. It had gone only a few yards inside the compound before being engulfed by jubilant kriegies who clambered on board and kissed the tank commanders and their troops without embarrassment. Some men ran past the tanks and over the debris where the gate had been. Tears of joy flowed as the liberated men roamed outside the barbed wire to experience a feeling they had been denied for such a long time—freedom.

A few minutes later, all eyes turned towards a church steeple standing in the center of Moosburg. It was later described by some of the liberated men as an event where 100,000 men wept. The despised, red and black, swastika-emblazoned flag of the Third Reich, seen by the kriegies every day, had been ripped down. In its place, the stars and stripes of the American flag were hoisted up the steeple and flapped briskly in the breeze. Some men snapped to attention and saluted Old Glory; others simply placed their hands over their hearts. The surge of patriotism began to heal a little of the anguish of the past months and years. They were no longer kriegies, prisoners, or POWs. They were free men, and they were on their way home.

From that moment on, the excitement was electric inside and outside the walls of Stalag VII-A. It was a massive and spontaneous international celebration involving over 20 different nations, all trying to grasp that their captivity was over. Foremost on everyone's mind was how quickly they could get home and how it would be arranged. Commanders of the Allied Forces told the men to try to remain as calm as possible while they waited to be transported out of Moosburg. There was no simple solution for liberating 130,000 POWs and returning them to their native countries. It would require patience, a quality that was difficult to ask of the anxious men after all they had been through.

Two days later, on May 1, 1945, General George Patton arrived at Stalag VII-A and was given an exuberant reception by the newly freed men. Dressed in a crisply laundered uniform, with a wide silver-buckled black belt, and his trademark ivory-handled six-shooters gleaming in their holsters, he was a sight for sore eyes. He

Jubilant Stalag VII-A POWs swarm one of their
liberator's Sherman tanks. April 29, 1945
Courtesy USAFA McDermott Library MS 329

was everything they imagined their liberator to be and more. He was
their savior—that was the word my father used. I don't recall when
in my childhood I first heard Patton's name mentioned or by whom,
but I do know that when I found out it was his Third Army that had
liberated my dad, he became an instant hero to me. In his story,
"The Liberation of Moosburg," Frank D. Murphy, a prisoner of war
at Stalag VII-A, recalled seeing General Patton stop to talk to some
of the liberated kriegies. He took one look at what German captivity
had done to the emaciated, filthy men and bellowed, "I'm going to
kill these sons of bitches for this."[18]

Some of the soldiers under Patton's command shared their K-
rations with the liberated prisoners. The Red Cross brought items
not seen or tasted by the men since they had become POWs, such
as freshly baked white bread, bacon, and eggs, which the starving
men greedily devoured. Many of them became violently ill, their
shrunken stomachs unable to digest the heavy, greasy foods. To
ease this problem, doctors and medics gave the men small liq-
uid-based meals several times a day, and as they became healthier,
slowly introduced solid foods back into their diets. There were also

Stalag VII-A POWs welcome General George Patton shortly after their liberation
Courtesy USAFA McDermott Library MS 329

sanitary issues to deal with; the latrines simply could not accommodate the number of men who needed to use them. The situation was
worsening and many of the men walked out of the camp to find their
own way back home, unable to deal with the squalid conditions any
longer.

My father had no intention of going off on his own. He knew the
Allied Command would work as quickly as possible to transport the
men out of Moosburg and resigned himself to the fact that he would
have to sit still until that happened. Like all the other POWs, he felt
the same overpowering joy for the first few hours of his freedom.
After that, the next 24 to 48 hours seemed like an eternity. He
needed to get word back home to Peggy and his parents that he was
alive and well, but there were no facilities to send telegrams, and
writing was out of the question: regular mail would take months.
He heard that sick prisoners would be the first group transported
out of Moosburg, followed by officers and finally, the enlisted men.
All he could do was wait.

On May 4, the wait was over. He boarded a troop transport truck
with eager, smiling ex-kriegies and took one more look back at

Stalag VII-A, hoping that someday he would be able to forget the weeks of misery spent there. The truck was bound for Landshut, Germany, about 20 miles northeast of Moosburg, where C-47 troop transport planes awaited them. Within hours, he boarded one of the aircraft and began the first leg of his journey home. He was on his way to Camp Lucky Strike in Le Havre, France.

It was late afternoon when the C-47 landed. The men disembarked and were led towards trucks that took them the short distance to their camp. Upon arrival, the tired and restless men jumped off the truck to get a closer look at what would be their final living quarters before returning to the States. As my father stared at the enormous tent city in front of him, he reached into his pocket and felt for Bobby's baby slipper. Tears of joy streamed down his face as he realized he had kept the vow he made nine months before when he lay bleeding in a grassy meadow in Austria. He had willed himself to survive and he had done it. Now it was time to go home to his wife and place their son's slipper next to the one she kept, so that once again they would be a pair, as he and Peggy would be for the rest of their lives.

Camp Lucky Strike was originally built as a staging area for Allied troops training for combat in the ETO. This camp and others in France were given cigarette names as a ploy to hide their locations from German intelligence.[19] Before the war, Le Havre had been a beautiful port city bustling with activity. In 1944, the Allies began their surge into western France, most notably on D-Day, June 6, at Normandy. Months later, on September 12, after intense fighting with the Germans, they secured the port of Le Havre. The result was costly, especially for the French locals. The city lay in ruins. Over the years, it had been the target of more than 150 bombing raids, earlier in the war by the Germans, and later by the Allies. A carpet bombing by the RAF ordered by General Montgomery on the night of September 5 leveled what was left of the city. If that was not enough to endure, the retreating Germans had destroyed most of the port facilities before they left.[20]

The British were the primary securing force at Le Havre, but they left shortly afterward in hot pursuit of the Germans. The Americans arrived soon after the Brits' departure and were faced with a huge undertaking. They had to rebuild the port facilities as well as deepen the sea channels to accommodate large naval vessels. On land, their job was even greater. They erected a huge tent city around the perimeters of Le Havre where they prepared their men for combat in western France and Germany. Many of the men trained there would see action in the storied Battle of the Bulge.

In the spring of 1945, Camp Lucky Strike underwent an enormous transformation. With the war's end coming, the emphasis shifted from shipping soldiers out to welcoming them back. By the end of the war, it was estimated that more than 3,000,000 troops either entered or left Europe through Le Havre; after the war, it was dubbed the "Gateway to America."[21] With the huge influx of ex-prisoners of war, the need for a debriefing and processing center was paramount. Almost all of the 130,000 POWs liberated from Moosburg eventually made their way to Camp Lucky Strike or other cigarette camps like it. My father was one of them, no longer a kriegie but a RAMP, the Allied military command's new moniker for all freed captives, which stood for Recovered Allied Military Personnel.[22] Thousands of RAMPs arrived daily, filthy and impatient to get shipped home.

My father's first order of business was to get word to Peggy that he was alive and safe. My mom was overcome with joy upon receiving two telegrams from Le Havre the first week in May. In addition to the wire my dad sent, the military also sent one, which read:

THE SECRETARY OF WAR DESIRES ME TO INFORM YOU THAT YOUR HUSBAND 2/LT KURTZ ROBERT R RETURNED TO MILITARY CONTROL 29 APR 45. ULIO THE ADJUTANT GENERAL.

After sending his telegram off, my father's priority was to get a hot shower. Although commanding officers did their best to sort out the myriad problems caused by the huge influx of RAMPs, it became obvious they could not solve them all. Causing the most angst were the agonizingly long lines. Everywhere my dad looked, lines of men snaked around Lucky Strike's tents, some with no end in sight. My father searched for the shortest line to the showers, knowing his efforts would probably prove futile. Eventually, with a shrug of his shoulders, he chose a random line and began the inevitable long wait. It would be hours before his first hot shower in over two months, but the wait would be well worth it. When he finally reached the head of the line, my father set aside all his personal items, stripped off his

foul-smelling clothes, and added them to a growing pile where they
would be later doused in gasoline, ignited, and reduced to ashes.

No one had a time limit for a shower or bath, and the RAMPs
scrubbed themselves raw. After toweling off, they were deloused
with DDT powder and one of them wrote that the men walked
around looking like someone had dumped a barrel of flour on them.[23]
Underwear, socks and shoes, fatigues, and army field jackets were
issued along with basic toiletries. It was the first clean clothing they
had worn in months. After getting dressed, they retrieved their personal items, and my brother's baby slipper found its way back into
the safety of my father's pocket. The men were then given a hot meal,
albeit a tiny one, and a few ounces of eggnog. As had been the case
in Moosburg, the Army doctors at Le Havre were concerned about
introducing solid food back into the men's diets. After their meal that
first night, they were assigned to tents. A clean cot with sheets and
blankets awaited them; for the exhausted men, it must have felt like
a luxurious bed in a five star hotel.

The next day was scheduled for debriefing and physical exam-
inations. One POW camp survivor perfectly describes both of those
processes:

> The following day we were debriefed (if you can call it
> that). We lined up by the hundreds in front of the GI
> clerks that had a typewriter on a small desk and a pile
> of one-page forms that gathered our vital information.
> This in my case covered name, rank, serial number,
> unit, date of capture, camp held in, and little else that
> I remember. Following that we were run through a
> physical that was in a like manner very superficial.
> The physical was a walk through and I was asked if
> I needed any medical help that couldn't wait till the
> States. I know of no POW that wanted anything but to
> get the hell out of there and home.[24]

It took hours of standing in long lines for debriefing and physi-
cals that lasted only minutes. Many RAMPs lied about their physical
status in order to be processed more quickly. Once they returned
to the States, those lies would come back to haunt them. Because
they had hidden their ailments from the attending doctors who
would have documented them, many were denied veterans benefits

because they could not prove their health problems were a result of their imprisonment.[25] It was a huge price to pay for impatience.

Once he had settled in, my father gathered up as much information as he could concerning the Advanced Service Rating Score, the point system that was used to determine which men would have priority to embark on one of the Victory ships waiting in the channels of Le Havre. Eighty-five points or more would assure him of a voyage in the near future:

- 12 points for each dependent child under age 18
- 1 point for every month of service in the Armed Forces, whether domestic or overseas
- 5 points for each combat award, including medals and battle stars[26]

He was excited about his chances for early departure; my father was drafted in 1941; a point for each month of service earned him close to 50 points. Add to that over a year overseas, his child back home, his Purple Heart and a couple other battle citations, and he was over the magic number and would be going home soon! Minutes later, my dad submitted his points for verification.

The following few days must have seemed endless. Reading had been my dad's saving grace in Stalag Luft III, but at Camp Lucky Strike he found it difficult to concentrate on the words in front of him. The weather was becoming warmer and he filled hours of time walking around the camp for exercise. He began to put weight back on and was regaining strength. On warmer days he basked in the sun, wanting to look tanned and healthy when he arrived home. "Home," no matter how many times my dad said the word, it always brought warmth and comfort. He would be seeing Peggy for the first time in over a year. He tried to imagine what Bobby looked like and how much he had grown. He would see his mom and dad and give them a huge hug. The harbor was filled with boats coming to retrieve homesick and war-weary soldiers and my father wondered which one would be his. The anticipation was almost too much to bear. On May 11, he wrote a letter to Peggy:

> *My own precious one, I sent two cables earlier in the week, darling, but haven't written before because we thought we were going right out. However, there's*

been a delay. I should be home with you and Bobby not later than the first of June, dearest, and I'm hoping and praying sooner. I wanted so much to be home for your birthday, baby, but we'll make up for it with a real celebration as soon as I get there. Have you read in the paper that we'll get a 60 day leave, sweet, there's so much we'll do, so much time to make up for. I can't wait to get home to you again. We're all on pins and needles waiting for our boat, every minute seems like a day. Oh, honey, it'll be so perfect. I can't wait to take you in my arms again, to be with you and Bobby every second, to show you both how completely I adore you. We'll make up for this past year, darling, we'll have a wonderful time! Bye for now, my baby, I'll be seeing you real soon. I love you with all my heart, soul, and body. Your very own, Bob.

Two days later, on May 13, the waiting was over. My father had been in Le Havre nine days when he was notified he would be on a Victory ship leaving for the States the next morning. He hurriedly sent one last telegram. Short and straightforward, its message was clear. The telegram arrived in White Plains on Mother's Day, and was the best present that my mother could have ever hoped for. Bob was on his way home!

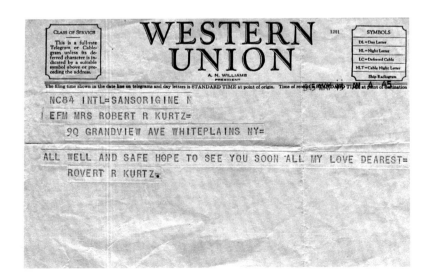

The next morning, my father gathered all his belongings and got on a bus that took him the short distance to the port of Le Havre. A few minutes later, he was looking at a huge troop transport ship that would be his ride home. Having dealt with so many endless lines at Camp Lucky Strike, he joined the long line that led to his boat, smiling as he figured he could deal with just one more. As he boarded the vessel, his heart began to pound until he thought it might explode from his chest. This was the last leg of his journey. In less than two weeks, he would run into the open arms of his darling Peggy. As the ship's horn blasted for departure, he prayed for a safe and uneventful voyage.

In spite of the fact that the ships were crammed to capacity with living conditions that left much to be desired, the next two weeks sailing across the Atlantic proved to be surprisingly therapeutic. The spring sea air and the exciting transition from a world of war to a world of peace helped calm nerves battered by months and years of combat and captivity. My dad chose to be top deck for most of the voyage, lounging in the sun during the day and gazing at the stars at night. Food was limited, but after all the men had been through in the POW camps, it was only an afterthought. Many dreamed of enjoying their first home-cooked meal sitting around the dining room table with their family and loved ones.

On May 28, 1945, fourteen days after departing the port of Le Havre, my father and hundreds of other soldiers wept openly as their ship sailed into New York Harbor and past the Statue of Liberty in all her splendor. They had fought for freedom and democracy, and had won.

RIPPLES

ON THE WAY BACK TO THE STATES FROM EHRWALD, I REalized that in three days I had learned more about my father than I had in the previous 50 years. My original intentions had been to seek out more about my dad's wartime experiences and find some type of closure for the void his untimely death had caused. I realized that finding information about my dad had not brought closure but rather an awakening, an opening to a whole new world filled with unanswered questions. My journey was not ending; it was just beginning. I made mental lists of people I wanted to visit back in the States who had known or trained with my father. If I had been hungry for information before this trip, now I was ravenous.

Mike and I touched down at Newark Airport and headed for customs. When the agent motioned me to step to the side and open my suitcase, he saw the twisted piece of wreckage from *Sugar Baby*, which looked ominous, like some type of crude weapon. I had laid it on top of my clothing, in full view, and the agent's eyes widened. He turned to me and said, "Mr. Kurtz, you better have a good explanation for this. If you can't give me a reasonable answer, I will have to confiscate it." After traveling thousands of miles and hiking thousands of meters, there was no way I was going to let that happen. I realized that the truth was my only option. "Sir," I said, "this is actually a piece of my father's co-pilot seat, which I pulled from the wreckage of his B-24 Liberator that crashed into the Austrian Alps during World War II." He was an older gentleman and may have served in the military, as many customs agents did. He not only believed my explanation, which was almost too crazy to have been invented, but was sincerely interested in my trip, and we talked about it for a couple of minutes before he allowed us to proceed.

When Mike and I arrived home, we spent the afternoon describing our trip to my wife and younger son, Brian. It was late summer and in a couple of weeks my sons would be back at college. The normal rhythm would resume, but my life was never going to be the same again. I had solved the mysteries of the majority of the contents of the green box, but my experiences in Ehrwald had opened up an entirely new field of questions. The next few years were busy ones, so I resigned myself to the fact that answering those questions would have to wait. Before long, my marriage ended in divorce. Living alone allowed for a lot of time for reflection, and I realized it was time to renew my efforts to discover more about my father's life. I began to contact people I had met in Austria, beginning with Debbie Beson. I planned a trip to Linwood, Michigan, to visit her and her family, where I would begin to see the ripples that my father's story had caused in the lives of others.

Debbie's father, Tony Jezowski, had invited me to visit him so that he could tell me firsthand what had happened in the deadly skies over Ehrwald, Austria, on August 3, 1944. After our climb to the Brendlkar in 2001, Debbie had told me that her father rarely spoke about his wartime experiences because the memories were too painful. So I was humbled by his decision to make an exception for me. He would soon be 80 years old, and WWII veterans were dying at a rate of more than a thousand a day.

As the date of my trip approached, I found it difficult to concentrate both at work and at home. I was about to meet the man whose life my father had saved. Tony Jezowski had gone on to live a full life: he had worked hard and raised a family, and was now enjoying retirement, none of which would have been possible if not for my dad's actions.

Debbie and her husband picked me up at the airport and on our ride back to Linwood we reminisced about our Ehrwald trip. It had been more than 20 years since I had last traveled to the Midwest, and I'd forgotten how flat the terrain was. Although Michigan was beautiful, I realized that living on the north shore of Massachusetts, near mountains and the ocean, had spoiled me. I knew Gerd Leitner had visited Debbie the year before, and he must have marveled at the absence of any type of elevation, having lived his entire life surrounded by the Austrian Alps.

We began the next day by touring the golf course that Tony owned and operated in Linwood. After lunch, Debbie brought me to her father's house. Her mom, Geraldine, met us at the door. She was a charming woman, petite and intelligent. She led us into the living room where Tony was sitting and as I approached, he stood up to greet me. I felt an instant connection to him. He was not a big man, but he exuded confidence. Wiry in appearance, he offered a bone-crushing handshake that attested to years of hard work developing his golf course. He was a hands-on type of man when it came to his business, deservedly proud of what he had accomplished.

As we sat down, Jezowski politely, though adamantly, insisted that our talk would be brief. He detested discussing his wartime experiences, from the moment he was shot down until his liberation from Moosburg. Tony's imprisonment at Stalag Luft IV had been horrific. Although controlled by the Luftwaffe, as was my father's camp, Stalag Luft IV's conditions were considerably worse for the non-commissioned officers. They were fed the same diet of saw-dust-filled black bread and green death soup, but the portions were significantly smaller. Debbie said that her dad always blamed the Germans for the digestive problems that he suffered with for the rest of his life. Tony said, "I still hold a grudge against the Nazis. Not because they shot me down, not because they held me in a POW camp, but because of the damned food, if you can call it that. Ruined my stomach for the past sixty years. I still can't look at a turnip or a piece of black bread."

As we settled back into the couch, Tony began the story I had been waiting so long to hear. "You know, Jim, I was not supposed to be on your dad's Liberator on August third, 1944. I was a member of an entirely different crew. We had been on R&R for a couple of days and Larry Hamilton, Charlie Sellars, and I were doing our best to enjoy it as much as we could. Three guys on your father's plane had been in a car accident the night of August second. They had a bombing mission scheduled for early the next morning and the flight com-mand at Pantanella was desperately looking for replacements. We all knew that a volunteered mission counted as two points toward the total of fifty that would get us home. Larry and Charlie jumped at the chance to add two missions to their number, but I wanted no part of it. I was thinking, 'Why tempt fate?' Command was looking to fill an engineer-gunner position, and that was my specialty. I told them to look everywhere for someone and if all else failed, I would go. At three o'clock in the morning, they were back for me and I joined your dad's crew. I was introduced to everybody and was happy to see Charlie and Larry there. We manned our positions, and took off for Germany to bomb a jet factory in Friedrichshafen."

Tony seemed to be getting a bit tired, so we took a coffee break; it was a short one, as he was anxious to go on. I wondered if relating the details of the air battle might prove to be therapeutic for him. He had carried the memories of that day for 60 years. I hoped this catharsis would help to chase away the demons of combat and death that had haunted him for so many years. Perhaps telling the story would bring him some peace of mind.

Jezowski continued, "The mission was a particularly tough one that day; our briefing had been right on. We were warned of intense flak and heavy German fighter presence over the target, and got more than we bargained for. Some of our bombers got pretty shot up and a few went down. We had a good run but our formation got broken up when we lost some planes. I had been worried about this all day because flight command told us we'd be flying 'tail-end Charlie.' It was always difficult to keep up with the formation when you were in that position. I found out later our squadron commander had swung too wide after bombing the target, which left us even more vulnerable. Fortunately, our bomber was not damaged severely and we began to relax a bit as we left the target area. But our pilot decided to hang back with some of the damaged planes to offer support, while the main formation kept on going and ended up several miles in front of us. Naturally, our fighters stayed with the main formation and we were left defenseless. I remember what happened next as if it was yesterday. We were flying in low cloud cover over the Austrian Alps when suddenly from underneath the clouds, thirty German fighters attacked our box formation of eight B-24s. We never had a chance. The firefight was intense. Our plane was taking hits from every direction and 20mm shells were ricocheting throughout the ship. I know for sure that I shot down at least one Me-109. Our B-24 took a direct hit and veered sharply. The two starboard engines were burning and we were spinning out of control. I had to get out of there fast. I jumped down from my gunner position and tried to put on my parachute but the cords were tangled up in the hanging wires. Most of the guys had already bailed out. I turned around and saw your father trying to beat out the flames on his pants before he jumped. He looked over at me and realized I was stuck, turned around, freed my cords, and we jumped out. Seconds later, the plane broke up in mid-air; we had just made it. Your dad saved my life."

When Tony was finished talking, he took a deep breath and stood up. I shook his hand and thanked him for allowing me to visit, knowing how very hard it had been to talk about that day. His story made me extremely proud of my father and I told him so. He acknowledged my pride with an understanding smile, the first one I had seen on his face since we had begun talking. A few minutes later, Debbie and I headed back to her house. I thanked her for arranging the meeting with her dad, and she, in turn, thanked me for allowing her to sit in on our conversation.

A few years later, Debbie shared some more stories about her dad so I could get a richer picture of his life after the war. Upon returning home from overseas, he met his wife, Geraldine, and they married in 1948. The engineering skills he had acquired in the Army Air Force proved indispensable when he started his own business, Tony's Trenching Service. He purchased the only hydraulic backhoe in the area to dig trenches. Some businessmen scoffed at the idea, positive that dirt would jam up the hydraulics and render the machinery useless. Jezowski knew better. His training had taught him that the hydraulic lines in the B-24 Liberator were kept free of dirt and debris by wiper rings. He knew the same concept would apply to his recently purchased backhoe, and while locals laughed at him, he laughed all the way to the bank. Years later in 1963, he opened up the Maple Leaf Golf Course, which he owned and operated for close to 50 years. Jezowski maintained that serving in the Air Force had taught him the engineering and management skills that

Staff Sergeant Anthony Jezowski
Courtesy Debbie Beson

made his business so successful. Debbie happily shared with me some words of wisdom her father had passed down to her and her siblings, such as: "If you don't understand how it works, you can't fix it," or "knowledge is power," a mantra he told his family he had developed after reading countless books as a POW. Debbie's favorite of his sayings was one she attributed to her dad's love of Linwood, and the fact that he had never lived anywhere else: "You've been searching for the bluebird in all the wrong places. It's been in your backyard the whole time!"

Anthony Jezowski was 91 years old when he passed away on September 14, 2012. I hope he meets my dad in the next world and, if he does, maybe they will exchange stories about their time in the Army Air Force. More likely, they will talk about their families and how much joy they had brought them. After the war, Tony spent more than 60 years bringing warmth, intelligence, and humor to the people around him. He lived a rich, full life. Rest in peace, Tony.

After spending time with Jezowski and realizing the profound effect that my father's life had had on his, I felt the urge to seek out

Top row, 2nd from left: Charlie Sellars; 3rd from left: Lawrence Hamilton;
2nd from right: Tony Jezowski. These three men formed the volunteer replacement crew for *Sugar Baby*. All others perished days later.
Courtesy Debbie Beson

more members of *Sugar Baby*'s regular crew. I found out that Lee Englehorn, the ball turret gunner, had passed away in 2003. I was under the impression that Joe Spontak, navigator on *Sugar Baby*, was the sole surviving crew member. But on my return trip to Ehrwald in 2010, Gerd Leitner told me that he was sure that bombardier George Britton was still alive. In the spring of 2011, a phone call from Joe Spontak brought wonderful news: Britton was very much alive and living in Boca Raton, Florida. I called George the next day and, though he was 86 years old and suffering from numerous ailments, he graciously invited me down to visit him. My quick response probably floored him. I asked, "Can I come tomorrow?"

Although he might not have been thrilled with my impetuous request, he seemed to recognize how important it was for me to hear his stories about my father, in person, as soon as possible. Encountering this kindness was my first insight into the warm and understanding man that George Britton was. I spent the evening writing down dozens of questions for him. Decades had passed since he and my dad flew together, so I wasn't expecting much detail. I was ready to listen to anything George could tell me; I knew he would open up another window into my father's life. As I pulled into his driveway, it felt like Christmas morning as a child, wondering what gifts I was about to receive, this time not toys, but treasured information about my father.

Doris Britton opened the door of their sun-filled Florida home and took me inside to meet her husband. He was sitting at a table, a black patch covering his right eye, and as he stood to shake my hand, I saw that he was a tall, powerful man, and soon found out he had a grip to match. I experienced the same sensation grasping his hand as I had the first time I met Joe Spontak in Austria. Shaking the hand of these two men, who must have done so with my dad hundreds of times during their service years together, was very moving. It was as if my father's hand was mine.

George had decided to wait until after dinner to talk, so we sat down to a delicious home-cooked meal of spaghetti and meatballs. The Brittons' two daughters joined us and our conversation was light-hearted and relaxed. After dinner we moved into the living room, and I pulled out my list of questions, but quickly realized how tedious this format was for him. Instead, I simply asked George if he had any distinct memories of my father that really stood out. I could see him searching his mind, trying to envision Bob Kurtz, co-pilot and good friend. Suddenly, a huge grin appeared on his face and he began, "Although much time has gone by, I do remember your father very well. He was a slightly built, soft-spoken man, always considerate, and he had a moderating influence on our more than difficult pilot. Many times, at the crew's request, Bob tried to talk sense into him. I can see your father's face most clearly. Officers' dress hats had a plastic strip to be snapped inside to keep them rigid, which was called a stay. I remember your dad always wore his dress hat without the stay. He took the plastic strip out and cocked the hat a bit sideways for the debonair look. If you look at our crew picture, you'll see what I mean. I can still see him sitting there in the co-pilot seat with his earphones over his hat. You can be proud of your father since he performed his duties well and we had total confidence in him. It was a frightening experience for all of us. You have probably seen WWII films of the bombing runs over Germany and know the tremendous courage it took for your father to sit there as co-pilot as the runs were made over the targets. The other distinct memory I have of your dad is that he was always concerned for his wife and son back home; since you were born after the war, you must have at least one older brother. I'm afraid that's about all I can remember about your father. I hope it was enough to make your trip down here worthwhile."

Worthwhile, indeed. I had listened to this wonderful man, my mouth wide open, as he shared his memories of my dad. How could I ever thank George enough? I didn't know it at the time, but a telephone conversation we would have months later would give me just the chance I needed.

After a quick break for dessert, Britton went on to tell his own story of the air battle over Ehrwald. He remembered the day of August 3, 1944, as one of sheer terror. With the two starboard engines engulfed in flames, he crawled out of his bombardier's position, opened the bomb bay doors, and bailed out. As soon as he exited the burning bomber, he questioned whether he had acted too hastily, wondering if the pilot or my dad had feathered the engines and extinguished the fires. Suddenly, he heard a plane motor. His lips trembled as he described what happened next: "I turned around to see a Focke-Wulf 190 fighter coming directly at me as I hung there helplessly. One small press of his finger on the gun trigger and I would be another victim of the savagery of war. I've often thought of that one second of fate that caused him to veer off at the last moment as I closed my eyes in fright. I floated down into a fir tree, crushing my left shoulder as a sharp branch entered my left thigh. I cut myself down, trembling, but alive." George paused, caught up in the memory, and began to wax poetic: "The valley seemed to belie the terrible air battle that had just taken place and its soothing greens and sharp stillness helped calm me down. I felt terribly alone in the vastness that surrounded me."

Britton then described how he immediately threw away his 45 automatic, just as my father had done, along with his bombardier wings, knowing that German soldiers would be swarming the area looking for the American airmen. He chuckled as he recalled the moment: "I was no Errol Flynn, and I was not prepared to be a hero." Soon afterward, George was taken prisoner. He went on, "There was a truck with other Americans waiting below. We were driven to the local police station and then marched to the Ehrwald train station, where I saw Lt. Crane, your dad, and Joe, the pilot, co-pilot, and navigator on our Liberator. I was relieved to see that my idiotic fear, that they had put out the fires and made it back to Italy, was baseless.

"The next time we were together was in Garmisch. Before being shipped out for interrogation at Dulag Luft, we were in a room in a building that served as a holding area. When I first saw them again, Joe was arguing with Lt. Crane as to why they had taken our plane to join the 'lame ducks' when we had miraculously made it through the flak-filled sky and should have stayed with the main fleet." George remembered the conversation almost word for word.

"Goddammit, Lieutenant, if you hadn't made that lousy decision we would have made it back," hammered Joe. "With no fighter protection we were doomed."

"I felt those poor bastards needed support, and we were in good shape," he argued.

"Yeah," continued Joe, "and we all would have gotten medals but instead we are going to sit on our asses as the war passes us by."

George smiled at me and said, "I felt just the opposite. I wouldn't have minded if the war had passed me by. I'd had enough. I felt lucky to have been shot down instead of being blown up, being killed by the flak or the fighters, or being burned to death as the plane fell to earth with the crew struggling against gravity to claw their way free." He confided that once he returned to the States after the war, ten years would pass before he would get up the nerve to fly on a plane again.

Sitting in his Florida home, 67 years later, Britton was still amazed that he had survived months of captivity in Stalag Luft III, as well as the Long March. His recollection of the transport of the prisoners in the cattle cars in Spremberg was particularly graphic. He never saw my father again after they were transported to Dulag Luft for interrogation, but his stirring descriptions of his time in captivity helped me envision what my father had endured.

We spent the last few minutes talking more about ourselves. Britton attended Columbia Business School after the war and worked for Colgate Palmolive in Paris, London, Vienna, and Zurich for 32 years, advancing to a high position in management. He lived in Europe from 1961 through 1982, at which point he retired. Both of his daughters were educated in Europe, a fact of which he was quite proud. They both married and moved to Florida within walking distance of Britton's home. He had three grandchildren, had recently celebrated his sixtieth wedding anniversary and, except for his health problems, seemed very content. I could see that he was getting tired, so I thanked him for his hospitality and his time. I stood up to shake hands but instead ended up in a heartfelt hug. I had a wonderful new friend.

Over the next year, I called Britton at least twice a month for additional bits and pieces of information. He was always happy to answer my questions and was astonished that not only was I interested in learning more about my father, but I was also committed to writing a book about him. One day on the phone, he asked me why I decided to call my book *The Green Box*. I explained that I had accumulated a lot of information about the contents of that box up in my attic throughout my life and was still doing so. While describing what some of those contents were, I told him that my favorites were my dad's wartime medals. I described how, as a young child, I would open up his Purple Heart and Air Medal cases and brush the medals' shiny surfaces with my tiny fingers. I asked about his citations and he told me that he had received the Air Medal and Prisoner of War Medal, but never received the Purple Heart. He reminded me of the shoulder injury he suffered after bailing out, and explained that the paperwork confirming his injury had been lost. Life had gone on after the war, and although he never forgot the omission, he never pursued it either. I asked if he still cared at this point in his life that he had not been awarded the Purple Heart. He replied that he had thought about it from time to time but that he simply didn't have the energy to follow it up. We hung up, and then suddenly an idea struck me. George may not have had the energy, but I certainly did. I had been looking for a way to thank him, and knew that if I could somehow pull it off, George Britton would receive the long-overdue recognition he unquestionably deserved. Come hell or high water, he would get his Purple Heart.

George was flabbergasted when I called him back and told him my plan. I asked for information that would be pertinent to obtaining his medal, such as his military dog tag number, the last four numbers of his social security number, and a description of the injury, along with when and how it had occurred. Finally, I needed the name of his congressman.

A couple of weeks later, armed with the necessary information, I began my lengthy conversation with government bureaucracy. My first call was to the office of Congressman Ted Deutch. When I described the situation to his secretary, she seemed genuinely interested in helping. Promising to relay my message, she gave me a contact in the War Record Department in Washington, D.C., who she thought might be of some assistance. A gentleman returned my call the next day and explained that there had been a massive fire in the war records building in St. Louis in the 1970s, where Britton's citation, along with almost all Army Air Force records from World War II, had been destroyed. He told me that without actual paperwork citing his injury, it would be virtually impossible to get George his medal. I was not going to give up that easily. I called Deutch's office and again spoke to his secretary about my predicament, explaining that George had a document written by a German physician at Stalag Luft III stating that he had been wounded in his right arm. I gave her Britton's telephone number and asked her to have the congressman call him directly. Another week went by without a word. With nothing else to lose, I decided on one last call to Deutch. I told him that George was 87 years old and in failing health. Even with an absence of records, why would a respectable veteran lie about his injuries just to obtain a medal? I pleaded with him to make it happen. Britton had surely earned his Purple Heart. Deutch promised to do whatever he could, but cautioned me not to be overly optimistic.

On August 18, 2012, George Britton was watching a Military Channel documentary on the history of the original Purple Heart commissioned by George Washington. He hit the pause button, went outside to get the mail, and could not believe his eyes. His Purple Heart Medal had arrived, along with a letter from the congressman's office, which read:

19TH DISTRICT, FLORIDA

COMMITTEE ON FOREIGN AFFAIRS

COMMITTEE ON THE
JUDICIARY

Congress of the United States
House of Representatives
Washington, DC 20515

1024 LONGWORTH HOUSE OF
WASHINGTON, DC 2
(202) 225-30C
WWW.DEUTCH.HOUSE

DISTRICT OFFICE
2500 NORTH MILITAR
BOCA RATON, FL 3:
(561) 988-630

MARGATE CITY H.
5790 MARGATE B
MARGATE, FL 33C
(954) 972-64C

TAMARAC CITY H
7525 NW 88TH A
TAMARAC, FL 33:
(954) 597-399

August 15, 2012

Mr. George Britton
5746 Wind Drift Ln
Boca Raton, FL 33433-5448

Dear Mr. Britton:

It is my honor and privilege to send you the Purple Heart Medal along with my thanks for your service to our country. Thank you for defending and fighting and keeping us safe. God Bless you.

Very truly yours,

Ted Deutch
Member of Congress

George Britton's Purple Heart letter
Courtesy George Britton

George H. Britton

Forever in our hearts

10.16.24 - 10.27.12

Courtesy Doris Britton

George called me right away with the good news. He told me that while placing his Purple Heart in a case with his war memorabilia, he was surprised to find two POW medals. A few months earlier, he had mentioned his prisoner of war citation; at that time, I wasn't aware that such a medal even existed. Apparently, every POW was awarded one, but for whatever reason, my father never received one. In a wonderful gesture of his own, George put his second one in the mail to me the next day. I was eternally grateful; it was the perfect addition to the green box and probably its last. That night I drank a celebratory glass of champagne, toasting George and our friendship. In some ways, he had become the father I had always yearned for. Two months after receiving his Purple Heart, George Britton passed away.

Staff Sgt. Charles Francis Sellars
Courtesy Debbie Cooke

BRINGING CHARLIE HOME

S INCE THAT LIFE-CHANGING VISIT TO EHRWALD IN 2001, MY
investigation into my father's past has continued to have a
rippling effect. My research touched the story of one crewman
who flew with my father that day, a story that needs to be told. The
crewman's name was Charlie Sellars.

I first heard his name on August 3, 2001, on that cold, rainy day
when I stood in front of a bronze memorial plaque with ten names
etched into its surface, 6,500 feet high in the Austrian Alps. The
plaque listed the crewmen of *Sugar Baby*. Tragically, the tail gunner,
who was severely injured during the battle, was unable to escape the
damaged aircraft before it crashed. As I knelt in front of the memorial,
I wiped the snow off the name of the airman who had met his maker on
that rocky mountainside, thousands of miles from his home. It read:
S/SGT Charles F. Sellars—Killed In Action.

Because he had been a replacement gunner on *Sugar Baby*, I
knew very little about Charlie Sellars. Then, during a return trip to
Austria with my fiancée, Julie, in 2010, I received a request from
Gerd Leitner, setting in motion a series of events that acquainted me
with Charlie Sellars in a way I would never have dreamed possible.

Our trip included a visit to Ehrwald, and another climb to the
Brendlkar on August 3, exactly 66 years to the day of the air battle
in 1944. Once again, Gerd Leitner offered to lead us up the mountain to the crash site. He also planned a visit to the local museum
and a meeting with Hilde Richter, a woman I had met in Ehrwald in
2001, who had photographs she was sure I would want to see. Gerd
mentioned that he, too, had something to show me and sounded very
excited about it in our e-mail correspondence, although he did not
reveal what it was. It was still a mystery when Gerd and his wife,
Elley, picked us up at the Garmisch train station.

We checked into Leitner's brother's hotel in Ehrwald, where
memories of my first trip to the village came rushing back. The next
morning, I showed Julie the monument to the air battle located in

the center of town. From there, we took a short walk to the local sporting goods store that Gerd owned, where we were fitted for the next day's hike. Elley joined us and we set off for our museum tour, led by Hilde's husband, who was the curator. The most touching item in the museum was a silk wedding gown that one of the local women had fashioned out of an American airman's parachute found in the valley the day of the air battle. She had hidden it until the war was over. The dress was simple but delicately sewn, and Julie held it up in front of her so I could take a picture.

Julie holding up the wedding dress

Back at the hotel, we sat down to lunch with Hilde Richter. In 2001, she had told me the story of how she, as a young girl, had been picnicking with her mother and brother the afternoon of the deadly battle over their tiny village. She witnessed my father's capture by German soldiers in the valley; her description of the event left no doubt that it was my dad she had seen. Her story had mesmerized me in 2001, and I couldn't imagine what she could possibly show me to top that. With a huge grin on her face, Hilde reached into her purse and took out two photographs of a little boy and girl standing with their mother in a valley on top of a boulder. She turned them over, revealing dates and inscriptions on the back. My mouth dropped open as I read: "3 Aug. 1944, Ehrwalder Alm." These were pictures taken minutes before a beautiful day for a picnic had turned into a day of death and horror. Gerd, who also joined us for lunch, said he recognized the spot and would take us there. A couple of hours later, he snapped a picture of Julie and me standing on the same boulder, just as Hilde and her family had done 66 years before.

After taking the snapshot, we prepared for our ascent to the crash site. Gerd finally revealed the surprise he had e-mailed us about— he handed me a gold wedding band. A local Ehrwaldian had given it to him a few weeks earlier, along with a story he had kept secret for nearly 70 years. Not long after the air battle, this same villager had been hiking in the Brendlkar when he came across the remains of *Sugar Baby*. He was combing the wreckage for souvenirs and while inside the burnt-out fuselage, he discovered a wedding ring and pocketed it. Decades later, he experienced a fit of conscience. Knowing that Leitner was one of the key organizers of the memorial ceremony in 2001, he gave the ring to him. Gerd asked whose ring I thought it was. I knew immediately that it had belonged to Charlie Sellars. Two of the three married crewmen on *Sugar Baby*, my father and John Cooper, had bailed out, been captured, and spent the rest of the war in POW camps where they were allowed to keep their wedding rings. That left only Sellars, who was killed in the air battle and went down with the plane. Leitner asked me to do whatever I could to return it to Sellars' closest kin and I promised I would do so.

When we returned home from our trip, I became a man on a mission. My first attempts to locate Sellars' immediate family on genealogy websites came up disappointingly empty. After three days, I was at my wit's end, ready to e-mail Leitner with the depressing news, when my cell phone rang. On the line was Brigadier General Jim Anderson, whose acquaintance I had made the year before at a business conference. He had called me just to say hello. I hadn't even thought of contacting him about my search for Charlie's family, but fate was on my side. I explained my predicament to him, hoping he might have some type of connection in the Department of the Army who could be of assistance, but, unfortunately, he did not. I figured I had reached another dead end, but right before we hung up, he remembered that the wife of a childhood friend of his, Carole Williams, had taken up genealogy as a hobby. Some of her work dealt with the military. He gave me her contact information and a shred of hope. I e-mailed her within minutes and included all of the information I had about Charlie's military service.

When I checked my e-mail the next morning, I couldn't believe my eyes. Carole had provided me with the names of three of Charles Sellars' living siblings with their addresses and phone numbers. Originally, my plan had been to return the wedding ring to Charlie's wife, Mary, but it turned out she had died in 1970. I called Charlie's younger brother, Ken, first. He was 79 years old and lived in Fulton, New York, only a few miles from Central Square, where the Sellars family had been raised on a rural farm. My initial conversation with Ken was a bit challenging, because I had to gain his confidence as to who I was and why I was calling. Sixty-one years had come and gone since they had buried Charlie. Now I was telling him I wanted to return his brother's wedding ring, which had been found at the crash site where he died. Ken's hesitant voice indicated that he thought it was some type of scam, but after a few minutes, he realized that my intentions were heartfelt and valid. He invited Julie and me to his home, and we arranged to arrive the following week; Ken wanted time to assemble family members to meet us and share our story.

Our five-hour drive from North Andover, Massachusetts, to upstate New York provided time for reflection. I was so pleased to be able to return the wedding ring to Charlie's brother. I also brought pieces of wreckage from the crash site, including the metal frame of a window that could possibly have held the glass in the tail gunner's position that Sellars had manned that day. Ken told me that his niece, Debbie Cooke, had always been interested in her Uncle Charlie's World War II experiences and had accumulated letters, telegrams, and war correspondence. Among them were inquiries that her grandmother, Anna Sellars, had written to the War Department, beginning from the time her son was declared missing in action. There also were letters sent to Anna from mothers and wives of the other nine crewmen on *Sugar Baby*, all eager for information on the whereabouts of their loved ones. Debbie had made copies of the correspondence for me and included a few photographs. I was bringing footage of the ceremony in Ehrwald in 2001, as well as of our climb to the Brendlkar and exploration of the crash site. As we approached Fulton, the excitement was building, and I had a feeling it was going to be a great day.

Ken and his wife, Janet, came out to meet Julie and me as we got out of our car. The rest of his family had not yet arrived so we took a quick tour of the house after our introductions. It was a warm, inviting home, and we were immediately comfortable with our hosts. It was impossible to contain my excitement any longer, and I reached in my pocket for Charlie's wedding ring. I handed it to Ken and for a moment nothing was said; nothing had to be. He shook my hand and thanked me. He had been around when his brother went off to war—old enough to remember him. On October 20, 1943, Charlie had returned on leave to his hometown to marry his sweetheart, Mary Eckert. Shortly afterward, he returned to training and eventually was shipped overseas. Ken had no idea on that day in October as he waved goodbye to his big brother at the train station that he would never see him again. The news of his death created a void in Ken's life that never left him. Feeling his brother's ring in his hand helped to ease his loss. He had a piece of Charlie back.

We quietly absorbed the moment. I pointed out to Ken that inside the wedding ring was the inscription "Orange Blossom," which I thought might have been Charlie's pet name for Mary but Ken wasn't sure. As it turns out, Orange Blossom was the name of a jewelry manufacturer established in the early 1900s that carried a wide range of merchandise.[1] The less pricey items could be found in most stores located near military bases, the perfect market because many of the soldiers moved up their wedding dates as they prepared to ship overseas, and their meager Army pay made the Orange Blossom wedding ring affordable.

A few of Ken's relatives began to arrive, and we went outside to greet them. I took *Sugar Baby*'s bent and rusted window frame from the trunk of my car and handed it to Ken. It looked like a piece of scrap metal that could be found in any junkyard, but when I explained what it was and where it had come from, it instantly became a treasured item. It was difficult for his family to fathom that the piece of rusted metal being passed around had been taken from the wreckage of Charlie's bomber. Ken especially loved it and immediately hung it in his garage, where it remains to this day.

We spent the rest of the afternoon and evening swapping stories and exchanging letters and photographs. I told them about the green box I had discovered as a child in our attic. I had brought some of the items with me, and explained the significance of each one. A bit later, I told them about the last day of Charlie's life—considerably more than they had known. It was difficult for me to describe the air battle in detail, especially the last couple of minutes after he had been injured, because he died such a horrible death in the skies over Ehrwald...but they obviously wanted to know everything. They knew Charlie had been a replacement gunner on *Sugar Baby*. Now it was Ken's turn to tell me something I had never known. His brother had volunteered to fly that day in order to get credited for two missions instead of one. On August 3, 1944, Charlie Sellars had 33 missions under his belt. He needed 35 to get his ticket punched back to the States; a successful mission would have accomplished that. I wondered how many times the same scenario had played out during the war. Charlie was 22 years old with so much to look forward to—a new wife, the opportunity to have children, raise a family, earn a decent living—all snuffed out in a matter of seconds. I mentioned to Ken how ironic it was that the two airmen killed that day, Charlie and Lawrence Hamilton, had both volunteered for the mission. Tony Jezowski was the third, but he survived. I wondered if they would have been better off remaining with their regular crew, so I asked Ken what he thought. He looked at me and shook his head. He explained, "Jim, you used the word 'ironic.' The reality is that if Charlie and the other two guys had not volunteered on August third, they would have lived only a few days more. The following week the rest of Charlie's crew was completely wiped out by a flak hit somewhere over Germany. I guess my brother and Hamilton's time was up, one way or another. Fate dealt just one good hand that day and it was to Tony Jezowski. He didn't want to fly on *Sugar Baby*, but he did because they couldn't find anyone else with his qualifications to be a replacement. If they had found someone, he would have remained with his original crew and been killed a few days later. Instead, he lived into his nineties. Now that, Jim, is truly ironic."

After dinner, we made plans for the next day. Ken wanted to show us the farmhouse in Central Square where he, his four brothers, and two sisters grew up. Julie and I wanted to pay our respects at Charlie's gravesite. I wondered how the next day's activities would affect

Ken. It was an outing that would take him decades into his past; some memories would be wonderful, others incredibly sad, but he seemed upbeat as we finalized the following morning's agenda. To end the evening, I suggested we watch the video my son Mike had taken of our trip to Ehrwald in 2001. All eyes of the Sellars family were glued to the television as I explained that they were watching the footage of the dedication of a memorial to the air battle of August 3, 1944. Tony Jezowski's granddaughter, Connie, was reading the names of the 30 American airmen who had lost their lives that day, her voice crisp and clear, echoing throughout the surrounding valley. When she read the name of Staff Sergeant Charles Francis Sellars, I looked around Ken's living room and saw the eyes of his family welling with tears. Minutes later, they watched our climb to the crash site and our exploration of the wreckage. It must have been extremely difficult to look at the exact location where their beloved Charlie had died. The video ended and Ken's family sat there stunned, not knowing what to say. His niece, Debbie, handed me the letters written by her uncle and grandmother. Before going to sleep, I read a few of them that Charlie had written home while in training and I was hooked. I couldn't wait to get home and read every one of them.

The next morning after breakfast, we hopped in my car, and with Ken as navigator, drove out to his childhood home. Ken told us that the house had been closed up for a few years; the current owners had died and occasionally a caretaker would come by to cut the lawn or feed the cat that still lived in the house. We followed the narrow driveway up to the farmhouse where Ken happily gave us a brief tour of the grounds. He had not been inside for several years. As he stood lamenting that fact, a pickup truck rumbled up the driveway and parked behind my car. My first thought was that a neighbor had called the police to report someone trespassing on the property. I approached the driver's side of the truck slowly, hoping my suspicions were wrong. Ken moved cautiously behind me, but when he recognized the property's caretaker, Bob, he relaxed. He introduced Julie and me and explained why we were all there. Ken was a bit hesitant to ask Bob if we could explore inside the house, even though I knew he really wanted to. I, on the other hand, viewed the situation as another surreal moment and knew I had to take advantage of it. The odds of the caretaker showing up at the farm on the only day we would ever be there were incredibly small, since he only worked four hours a month there. Not wanting to pass up the perfect opportunity, I askcd Bob if we could go inside. His next words were music to our ears. "Sure guys, take as long as you'd like; I've got a few things to do outside on the property. These people never threw anything away, so it's a little tight in there. Be careful walking around and try not to step on the cat."

We entered through the kitchen, as Charlie must so often have done. Having been closed up for so long, it was a bit like a ghost house, musty smelling, with thick dust on every surface and cobwebs in all the corners. Ken's memories of his childhood began to flow. "We spent a lot of time in this kitchen. Mom was a real good cook. I can still smell her fresh baked cookies! I remember us all sitting down for supper shortly before Charlie went off to war. The table was over there, and I can see my brothers and sisters as if it were yesterday: Billie, Charlie, Eddie, Paul, myself, Ethel, Carol, and, of course, Mom and Dad. Right after grace was said, it was everyone for themselves. We always had enough to eat, but with six siblings you wanted to make sure you got your share."

Ken showed us around the first floor and I wondered what it had been like to grow up with nine people in the same house, so I asked him. He replied, "To tell you the truth, I don't ever recall it being a problem. We had plenty of room and everybody had their chores, whether indoors or out in the fields. We stayed out of each other's way and got our jobs done. Fact is I embraced the warmth and comfort of our home."

We decided not to go upstairs, but Ken gave us an idea of how many bedrooms there were and how they were shared. Preparing to leave, we headed back through the kitchen when Ken stopped abruptly and turned around, realizing that, in all likelihood, this would be his last time inside his childhood home. He wanted to share one final memory with us. "I remember Charlie sitting at the dinner table in full dress uniform. He looked so proud and dignified. I was in total awc of him. Charlie was my hero. I didn't want him to go off to war, but I knew he had to, and I'll never forget saying goodbye to him."

It was quiet as we drove off the property, Ken reflecting on his past that had been filled with so many rich memories, and me still incredulous that the caretaker had arrived at just the right moment to let us in. I had enjoyed watching Ken's facial expressions and his reactions as he walked through the farmhouse, moving from room to room, talking about the life he remembered there. We had been extremely fortunate to have joined him on a deeply moving journey back in time.

Ken looked back one more time as we drove down the driveway and wistfully commented, "It was all so much simpler back then."

In a letter Anna Sellars received from her son on March 15, 1943, Charlie had written:

At this very moment, I could go for about three dozen of those delicious cookies, Mom. I'm hungry as a bear.

That spring, PFC Charles Francis Sellars was an Army Air Force cadet stationed at Keesler Air Base, Biloxi, Mississippi. In the same letter, he described the rigors of basic training. Calisthenics, flight training, and classroom instruction dominated his waking hours, leaving little leisure time for writing home. The letter's postscript read:

I'll be glad when this damn war is over with so people can go back to living normally again. Keep your chin up, Mom, it will be over soon.

There were 21 letters in all. The first one was dated February 3, 1943, and postmarked Biloxi. The last was sent from Pantanella, Italy, on July 31, 1944, and was not postmarked because all overseas mail from battlefronts had to be censored. Charlie and his B-24 crew flew daily bombing missions into Germany and their Army Air Force base locations were classified information.

The letters sent home while he trained in the States are repetitive, painting the picture of a grueling training schedule in less-than-comfortable conditions. Charlie's first months of gunnery school and flight training were in Mississippi and Texas from June to September, 1943. The heat was stifling. He wrote:

Here it is Monday morning, mom and hot as usual. I'll bet it is just about right up there isn't it mom? As I am sitting here writing this letter my whole body is dripping with sweat.

All three pages of this letter were splattered with perspiration, smearing the ink so much that parts were unreadable. The food left much to be desired and Charlie pulled no punches in its description:

> *We have had horse meat quite frequently. It don't taste too bad but I'll bet that hunk of meat I had today came off a nag that pulled a double plow for 8 years because I thought I had a mouthful of horseshoe nails.*

One interesting letter was written to his mother trying to explain why he had chosen the Army Air Force over other branches of the service, in response to a letter she had written voicing concerns for his safety. After reading statistics on mortality rates of bomber crews, in training and in combat, she was frantic. Charlie responded:

> *Nothing possessed me for going into flying, mom. All there is to it is the fact that those physically fit are sent to gunnery school whether they like it or not. It's not hard to wash out of it but that's not for me unless I'm incapable of shooting accurate enough to pass. Mom, I wouldn't have gotten any closer to home if I wasn't in gunnery because all the rest of the boys that didn't pass are out in Salt Lake City in Utah.*

Charlie's interest in current events wove a common thread through almost every letter he sent home. In January of 1944, he wrote from McCook Air Base, Nebraska, giving his perspective on the war in Europe and why he felt Hitler's methods would fail, and revealing a bit of the propaganda that was part of his training:

> *They sure are squeezing Hitler, mom. He may have a big army mom but what good is an army if they haven't any equipment and they're freezing from lack of clothing and not only that but the morale is at a very low ebb.*

In the same letter, he continued his own analogy of the situation:

> *It's just like a gambling game, mom. A guy can start out winning one game right after the other but as*

*soon as he gets to think he can never be beat, he be-
gins to lose his shirt and that's just what's happening with Hitler. He is afraid of that invasion rumor.
That's why he doesn't dare put his full amount of forces against the Russians. Now what I'm waiting to see
is the Nazis getting driven out of Italy.*

The last batch of letters was from Pantanella. The young airman
was flying combat missions almost every day, but he still kept up
with the news on the battlefront. Anna Sellars had no idea where in
Italy her son was stationed, but she was well aware of the dangers he
faced every day. Upon hearing of the Allied invasion at Normandy,
the next day, June 7, 1944, he wrote his mother and he sounded
excited:

*A happy good afternoon to you, mom. How are you
feeling this fine P.M.? Fine and dandy I hope. I am
feeling in the best of health and good spirits, mom.*

Further along in the same letter, his mood soured a bit when a pang
of homesickness hit him:

*Gosh here it is almost summer already. I'll bet the
kids head for the pond pretty often now, don't they,
mom? I haven't been swimming since the summer of
1942. I guess I will need to take swimming lessons all
over again.*

On the last page, his thoughts returned to the invasion:

*Speaking of the war, mom, things look brighter all
the time. Cherbourg has been seized, the boys are in
high gear in northern Italy, and the Russians are advancing.*

By late July, Charlie had flown more than 25 bombing missions
and was getting closer to the magic number of 35 that would allow
him to return to the States. It was July 21, a Saturday morning on
one of the rare days he was not scheduled to fly, and he was listening
to the radio, trying to relax when he wrote:

Our radio is on at the present moment, mom, and some of that good American music is on. It kinda brightens up the atmosphere around here in the a.m. The news just came on, mom, and it was broadcasted that Hitler narrowly escaped assassination but didn't miss some of his staff. Too bad, too bad. Things must be in somewhat of a turmoil inside Germany. Things look brighter and brighter as the days go by and it won't hurt my feelings when it all comes to a screeching whoa.

As July ended, Charlie wrote his mother a letter that turned out to be the last piece of correspondence she would ever receive from him. It began:

Dear Mom and all at home, Here it is the last day in July somewhere in Italy, mom, and it is beginning to get pretty warm already this a.m. I received your grand letter of July 21 and sure am happy to hear from you, mom. Everything is going on the same as usual over here. All the forces on the Allied fronts are squeezing Hitler and his tribe tighter and tighter. I don't imagine the Germans will be doing so well if it is true Rommel is out of commission.

His last words to his mother were:

I am at the end of the sheet, mom, so will have to close now. I will write soon. All my love, Charlie.

There would be no more of Charlie's letters arriving at the home of Anna Sellars. At the time of his final letter, he had flown 31 bombing missions and would fly an additional two in the following couple of days. On August 3, 1944, on a beautiful Friday morning, he was killed in action, an hour before completing what would have been his last mission.

On August 17, Anna Sellars received a telegram from the War Department signed by J.A. Ulio, Major General, the Adjutant General, stating that her son had been reported missing in action since August 3. It was a form telegram that assured the next of kin that every possible means would be taken to obtain information as to the status of the missing soldier. From that day on, Anna Sellars, along with thousands like her across the country who had received similar telegrams, began an agonizing waiting period full of fear, hope, and unanswered questions. Were their sons alive? If so, had they been injured? Accounts of lethal air combat during bombing missions that Sellars' mother had read about had become terrifyingly real and they haunted her. Anna knew that if Charlie had survived being shot down, there was a good possibility he would eventually end up in a prisoner of war camp. If that was the case, it might be months before the International Red Cross would send her a telegram naming the location of the camp and word that he was alive. There was nothing she could do but wait. She still had another son serving overseas, five children at home to take care of, and a house to keep up. Even with so much to do, Anna never stopped thinking about Charlie.

In mid-August, Anna Sellars sent the first of many inquiries to the War Department, desperately seeking information about her son. She saved every response. The first one, written on September 27, came from the Headquarters of the Army Air Forces in Washington, D.C., from C.A. Oakley, 1st Lt. A.C., Notification Branch, Personal Affairs Division. It read:

```
Dear Mrs. Sellars, I am writing you with
reference to your son, Staff Sergeant
Charles F. Sellars, who was reported
missing in action over Germany since
August 3rd. Further information has
been received which indicates that
Sergeant Sellars was a crew member of
a B-24 Liberator bomber which departed
from Italy on a bombardment mission to
Friedrichshafen, Germany on August 3rd.
Full details are not available, but the
report further indicates that during
this mission en route from the target, at
about 11:35 a.m., our planes encountered
hostile aircraft. During the battle
several damaged bombers were observed
in the vicinity, however, it could not be
determined whether one of them was your
```

son's plane. A number of parachutes were also seen in the vicinity but it is not known from which planes they emerged. Due to necessity for military security, it is regretted that the names of those who were in the plane and the names and addresses of their next of kin may not be furnished at the present time. Please be assured that a continuing search by land, sea, and air is being made to discover the whereabouts of our missing personnel.

It would be two excruciating months before Anna would receive any additional correspondence concerning her son. Every hour felt like a day, every day like a week. Finally, on November 26, a letter arrived from Adjutant General Ulio. It was not good news.

As promised you, I am writing again regarding your son, Staff Sergeant Charles F. Sellars, 12-167-679. It has been my fervent hope that favorable information would be forthcoming and that you might be relieved from the great anxiety which you have borne during these months. It is therefore with deep regret that I must state that no further report in his case has been forwarded to the War Department. I want to again emphasize the fact that the Commanding Generals in all our theaters of operations are making a continuous effort to establish the actual status of personnel who have been reported as missing, or missing in action. In many instances the War Department must rely upon the reports by a belligerent government through the International Red Cross for information. In the event no additional information is received within the next three months, I will again communicate with you.

On December 1, Anna Sellars received a communication from Colonel Clyde V. Finter, chief of the Personal Affairs Division at Army Air Forces Washington, D.C. headquarters, which allowed her to widen the search for information concerning her son. He wrote:

> Dear Mrs. Sellars: For reasons of military security it has been necessary to withhold the names of the air crew members who were serving with your son at the time he was missing. Since it is now permissible to release this information, we are enclosing a complete list of names of the crew members. The names and addresses of the next of kin of the men are also given in the belief that you may desire to correspond with them.

This letter gave Charlie's mother new hope. She now had the names of the next of kin of nine crew members. Only the names of Anthony Jezowski and Lawrence Hamilton were familiar. Hoping that someone on that list had heard from their sons or husbands, and might have news of Charlie, she immediately sat down and wrote to each one. The remaining crew members' families had received identical information from the War Department in early December, spawning a flurry of correspondence totaling 90 letters. Every airman's family received nine letters from each of their crew's next of kin. Some had already been notified of their loved ones' whereabouts by the International Red Cross; others were still in the dark. All of the letters were supportive in nature, with every one trying to be as positive as possible.

As I read through the letters that Anna Sellars received, three of them stood out. The first of these was typewritten and was from my mother. It was hard for me to believe I was holding a copy of a letter she had written 66 years before. Although formal in appearance, the contents were anything but, as she warmly reached out to a woman she had never known. On December 12, my mom wrote:

> *Dear Mrs. Sellars, I just received your letter today and wanted to write right back to let you know what we have heard. I have several friends who have been*

*forced down over enemy territory and are now pris-
oners. However, more times than not, it has taken
nearly six months before they have been heard from.
In this way, I feel that you will no doubt hear something soon. Perhaps your son landed several miles
from some of the others and was able to escape being
taken prisoner and is with the underground as happens so many times. Also, I would like to think there
was a good chance that he may be a prisoner, but
the official word has not gotten through to you yet.
Sometimes the German government is very slow in
releasing that information. I realize that you have already heard this all many times before, but it is very
true and I thought it might help during this period of
waiting which I know from experience is so terribly
hard. I sincerely hope you hear good news real soon
and will let me know right away and with this hope,
I remain sincerely yours, Margaret L. Kurtz.*

The second letter Anna received, dated December 13, was from Mary Britton, mother of bombardier George Britton. Like my mother, she had never met Mrs. Sellars, but she reached out to her with words of encouragement and hope. She wrote:

*We had a letter from the pilot's father last week say-
ing that he met some boys that came back from their
squadron. I was told that the plane they were in came
down in the Alps and that the ten chutes were seen
opening, so probably the boys got separated or perhaps your son got away and wasn't taken prisoner
and can't let you know just yet where he is. We have
heard of so many cases like that, it takes a little longer, but I am sure he will turn up alright. We feel so
sorry for you, the suspense was awful until we were
notified on the 5th of Sept. George was alive, we were
nearly crazy.*

Mary Britton had unintentionally given Charlie's mom renewed hope that he might still be alive if, indeed, ten chutes had been seen exiting the burning bomber. She clung to that belief for several more months until the debriefing of *Sugar Baby*'s crew after their

BRINGING CHARLIE HOME

liberation confirmed that pilot Crane's father had been given false information. Not all ten parachutes had descended from the B-24; Charlie was unable to jump to safety and went down with the plane.

The most gut-wrenching letter was from Lawrence Hamilton's mother, Regina. Hamilton had been one of Charlie's original crew and had trained with him for months before being shipped overseas. Anna and Regina shared one horrible similarity—information on both of their sons was still unavailable in mid-December. The whereabouts of the other eight crewmen had all been determined; they were prisoners of war in either Stalag Luft III or Stalag Luft IV. On December 14, Mrs. Hamilton wrote from Louisville, Kentucky:

> *Dear Mrs. Sellars, I read your letter and was much pleased to hear from you. Was sorry you had not heard from Chas. I know just what suspense it is to wait for I too have had no news. I have heard from Mr. Crane, Mr. Spontak and the Coopers and each of their sons are POWs. I can't see why we can't hear from our sons. If they are O.K. and with the underground I realize they are much better off and won't be able to let us hear from them. Even if I can't hear from Lawrence I do hope he is not injured or being halfway-fed. Of course I am interested in all the boys on the crew but especially Chas. and Tony Jezowski as the three were of the original crew and have been pals a long time since training in the States. I certainly do hope we have some good news from our sons soon. Best wishes for a Merry Christmas to you and your family, Mrs. Regina Hamilton.*

The anguish in her every word is palpable. She and Anna Sellars became steadfast friends for all the wrong reasons, suffering through the holidays and for several more months, hoping beyond hope that by some miracle their boys were still alive.

On March 20, another letter from the War Department arrived at the Sellars home. It was from Major General Ulio, fulfilling his promise to contact Anna at the end of three months with additional information on Charlie's status. The beginning of the letter must have sent her to her knees:

It distresses me to have to inform you that no report of any change in his status has yet been received. If at the expiration of twelve months a missing person has not been accounted for, all available information regarding the circumstances attending his disappearance is reviewed under the provisions of Public Law 490, 77th Congress, as amended, at which time a determination of his status is made. The War Department is mindful of the anguish you have so long endured and you may rest assured that, without any further request on your part, you will be advised promptly if any additional information concerning your loved one is received. Should it become necessary to establish his status in accordance with the provisions of the law cited, you will be notified of the findings shortly after the expiration of the twelve months' absence. You have my heartfelt sympathy in your sorrow and it is my earnest hope that the fortitude which has sustained you in the past will continue through this distressing period of uncertainty.

Anna Sellars never lost hope that her son had somehow survived, but this correspondence from Ulio had a demoralizing effect on her, and although she tried to shake the negative thoughts running through her head, the letter in her hand delivered a cold and clear message. In five months, her son would be officially declared dead, killed in action. It was a message she could not and would not accept.

Two days after Ulio's letter, Anna received word from Lawrence Crane's mother describing the comfort of knowing that her own son was alive, and suggesting how Mrs. Sellars should handle her uncertainty concerning Charlie. Mrs. Crane wrote:

We haven't received Larry's clothing nor all his personal things. The other day the Air Medal came. This all tends to make one sad but also close to our dear boy. Mrs. Sellars, we won't say Charlie is gone. He is just busy in the other room, for a while perhaps. Try to think of him as just in the other room out of sight only. It helps. Bless him and you too.

Three more months passed without updates on her son, ten months since the first communication from the War Department, and Anna's hopes that Charlie had somehow survived were fading. Finally, she received a letter from *Sugar Baby's* pilot, 1st Lt. Lawrence Crane, with the news that every mother of every soldier fighting on battlefronts around the world prayed they would never receive, and erasing any doubt as to the fate of her son. Written on June 27, 1945, it read:

Dear Mrs. Sellars, Arriving home late last night, I thought I must write you and Mrs. Hamilton first thing this morning in case you have not heard it from someone else already. The bombardier and engineer, George Britton and Ed Bracken, told me after our capture, that your son, Charles, was killed in his tail turret instantly by enemy fire. It is with deep regret that I tell you this and pray you will take it like the soldier Chas. was. Please let me hear from you. Lawrence Hamilton is still missing and we are all praying to hear from him.

Crane's letter devastated the Sellars household, especially Anna, who had never given up hope through months of uncertainty. She wrote to the families of the crew members on Charlie's bomber, most of whom had just arrived home from overseas after months spent in prisoner of war camps. She needed to know more about her son's death and the minutes leading up to it. Perhaps Britton and Bracken had been mistaken. She begged for news. Two weeks later, she received a response from Leonard Bracken, the engineer who had flown with him that ill-fated day. Though he had only known Sellars for a few hours, he wrote to Charlie's mother to offer his condolences. On July 8, 1945, from Chattanooga, Tennessee, Bracken wrote:

Dear Mrs. Sellars, I'm terribly sorry if I mess this all up. I never did anything quite like this before and

I hope I never have to again. I'm very much afraid that Lt. Crane is right. Your son never got more than maybe seventy-five rounds off before they got him. You can always be very proud of your son. He went down fighting, like the man he was. Although I didn't know him too well, as you know he was a substitute on our crew that day, I did know him well enough to know he was a fine boy. I'm afraid I'm just making it harder for you. I just want you to know you have my deepest sympathy. Yours very sincerely, S/Sgt. Leonard E. Bracken.

Five months later, on August 4, 1945, the letter Anna Sellars had hoped would never come, yet knew must, arrived at her home. It was from Major General Edward F. Witsell, acting Adjutant General of the War Department:

Dear Mrs. Sellars, Since your son, Staff Sergeant Charles F. Sellars, 12-167-679, Air Corps, was reported missing in action 3 August 1944, the War Department has entertained the hope that he survived and that information would be revealed dispelling the uncertainty surrounding his absence. Full consideration has recently been given to all available information bearing on the absence of your son, including all records, reports, and circumstances. These have been carefully reviewed and considered. In view of the fact that twelve months have now expired without the receipt of evidence to support a continued presumption of survival, the War Department must terminate such absence by a presumptive finding of death. Accordingly, an official finding of death has been recorded under the provisions of Public Law 490, 77th Congress, approved March 7, 1942, as amended. I regret the necessity for this message but trust that the ending of a

long period of uncertainty may give at
least some small measure of consolation.
I hope you may find sustaining comfort
in the thought that the uncertainty with
which war has surrounded the absence
of your son has enhanced the honor of
his service to his country and of his
sacrifice.

The day after receiving the correspondence declaring her son
dead, Anna vowed she would do everything in her power to bring
Charlie's remains home for proper burial. Though she was strong-
willed and persistent, Anna received a letter from Captain Donald
S. Gibson, Air Corps Chief, Casualty Unit, in early September of
1945, containing disheartening news that for a while caused her to
abandon the quest to bring Charlie home. Stationed in the Personal
Affairs Section at Rome Air Technical Service Command at Rome
Army Air Field in Rome, New York, close to the Sellars home, Gibson
wrote:

Dear Mrs. Sellars: When I called at your
home a few days ago concerning your son,
S/Sgt. Charles F. Sellars, I promised
to write to the Quartermaster General,
requesting information as to the details
of burial of your son. However, when I
sat down to write the letter I discovered
that your son was carried as "Missing
in Action", from 3rd day of August 1944
until the 4th day of August 1945. As no
information concerning him was received
during that year's period, he was, on
the latter date, presumed to be dead in
accordance with provisions of Section 5,
of the Act of 7 March 1942, (Public Law
490, 77th Congress). This would mean that
the body of your son has not been located
and, therefore, the Quartermaster General
could have no information concerning the
burial your son received. I am sorry
that I cannot obtain the information

> for you that you desire. I appreciated
> the opportunity of talking with you and
> Mrs. Mary Sellars. May I again extend my
> deepest sympathy in your bereavement.

Letters and conversations with Charlie's crew members the following months helped to determine the general area where their B-24 Liberator had crashed. Anna knew her son had gone down with the plane somewhere in the Austrian Alps. Beyond that, she was helpless in her efforts to locate where Charlie had been buried or if he had been buried at all. Desperate for any type of closure, she refused to give up. In previous correspondence, a letter from Major General Witsell had designated August 4, 1945, as a presumptive date of death by Public Law Provision 490, because the whereabouts of Charlie's remains were still unknown. Almost a year later, on May 15, 1946, Anna's husband, Maitland, received a letter from Witsell offering new hope that his son's body might be found. He had acquired additional information and forwarded it to the Sellars home:

> An official report based on information
> obtained from captured German records
> has now been received that he was killed
> in action on 3 August 1944 near Ehrwald,
> Germany. Pursuant to the provisions of
> Public Law 490, 77th Congress, 7 March
> 1942 as amended, official reports will now
> be issued by the War Department which
> will indicate the actual date of his
> death as that shown above.

Sellars' death status was now cleared up, but the whereabouts of his body was still in question. To make matters more confusing, Major General Witsell had mistakenly identified Ehrwald as a German town. Anna was not even sure where to continue the search for her son's remains.

Four years passed without any further information, though Anna and her daughter-in-law, Mary Sellars, still actively sought to bring Charlie back home. Then, in 1949, a letter arrived at Mary's home from the office of the Quartermaster General in Washington, D.C. Written by Major James F. Smith of the Memorial Division, it would provide the answers both women had waited so many years to hear:

Dear Mrs. Sellars, We are desirous that you be furnished information concerning the resting place of the remains of your husband, the late Staff Sergeant Charles F. Sellars. The official report of burial has been received and discloses that the remains of your husband were originally buried in an isolated grave located at Ehrwald, Austria, but were later disinterred by our American Graves Registration Personnel, properly identified, and reinterred in Plot IIII, Row 4, Grave 48, in the United States Military Cemetery St. Avold, located twenty-three miles east of Metz, France. The report further indicates that these remains have now been casketed and are being held at the cemetery pending disposition instructions from the next of kin, either for return to the United States or for permanent burial in an overseas cemetery. According to our records, identification of the remains of your husband was established by the favorable comparison of tooth charts made for the deceased with those maintained in Army dental records for your husband. The color of the hair of the deceased is also in agreement with the color of your husband's hair as shown on his Army records. In addition, the estimated date and place of death, as given on the official report of burial, is in agreement with the records of the adjutant General's Office of your husband. There are inclosed information pamphlets regarding the Return of World War II Dead Program, including a Disposition form on which you may indicate your desires in this matter. In order that this office

> may take immediate action toward the
> final disposition of the remains of your
> husband, it is urged that you complete
> the inclosed form and mail it to this
> office without delay. May I extend my
> sincere sympathy in your great loss.

All that remained was a massive amount of paperwork. Burial in a military cemetery in Europe was out of the question. As far as Anna and Mary were concerned, Hillside Memorial Cemetery in Central Square would be his final resting place. Mary Sellars received a telegram from a Brooklyn Distribution Center a few months later with the specifics:

> PLEASE BE ADVISED THE REMAINS OF THE LATE S SGT. CHARLES F. SELLARS ARE EN ROUTE TO THE UNITED STATES. OUR RECORDS INDICATE YOU WISH REMAINS DELIVERED TO YOU AT THE ABOVE ADDRESS. WE CANNOT GIVE YOU A DEFINITE DELIVERY DATE. IT IS EXPECTED THAT AN INTERVAL OF SEVERAL WEEKS WILL ELAPSE BEFORE DELIVERY CAN BE EFFECTED. YOUR FUNERAL DIRECTOR WILL BE NOTIFIED BY TELEGRAM THREE DAYS PRIOR SHIPMENT OF REMAINS FROM THIS DISTRIBUTION CENTER OF DATE AND TIME REMAINS WILL ARRIVE AT RAILROAD STATION. PLEASE ARRANGE WITH YOUR FUNERAL DIRECTOR TO ACCEPT REMAINS AT RAILROAD STATION. HE WILL BE REQUESTED TO INFORM YOU SO YOU MAY MAKE FINAL FUNERAL ARRANGEMENTS. REMAINS WILL BE ACCOMPANIED BY MILITARY ESCORT. SUGGEST YOU ARRANGE WITH LOCAL PATRIOTIC OR VETERAN'S ORGANIZATION IF YOU DESIRE MILITARY HONORS AT FUNERAL.

A few months later, Staff Sergeant Charles Francis Sellars made his last journey; he did not return to the United States alone. An article in the Syracuse *Post-Standard* on August 9, 1949, stated that 1,209 remains had been sent to a New York Port of Embarkation on a mortuary ship named *Carroll Victory*. Upon arrival, they were transported in special mortuary railroad cars under military guard to Distribution Center #1, their last stop before arriving home.

As we drove to the cemetery, Ken pointed to the American Legion Post, where he was a well-respected member. Serving in the military was important in the Sellars family; Ken had fought honorably for his country in Korea and was extremely proud of his service there.

Our final stop was Hillside Memorial Cemetery. Walking toward the grave, we talked about the letters his mother and sister-in-law had written to the War Department during their drawn-out and painful efforts to bring Charlie's remains home. Suddenly, Ken stopped, and there at our feet was his brother's headstone. It read:

CHARLES F. SELLARS
NEW YORK
STAFF SGT. 465 AAF BOMB GROUP
WORLD WAR II
MARCH 23 1922   AUG 3 1944

We silently paid our respects, then drove quietly back to his home, deep in our thoughts.

Charlie Sellars came home for the last time in early fall and was buried on a hilltop overlooking the farmlands of Central Square. The leaves had just begun to change; the autumnal foliage with its vivid reds, oranges, and yellows was glorious. Charlie would have loved it.

Ken Sellars kneels in remembrance at his brother Charlie's grave

The Kurtz Family
February 1952

WHITE PLAINS 1945–1952

MY FATHER ARRIVED STATESIDE, WAR-WEARY AND ANXious to get on with his life. He had lived through nine months of hell. As the crowded troopship eased slowly past the Statue of Liberty, he reflected on his homecoming. His saving grace and the reason he had survived was waiting for him... Peggy. He knew she would be holding one of Bobby's slippers and he squeezed its counterpart tightly in his hands, assured now that their pact to reunite them was only minutes away. Somehow, he would try to forget what had happened thousands of miles away. It was nearly lunchtime and his stomach rumbled. How many times in the last nine months had he felt those same hunger pangs and been unable to alleviate them? But the loneliness had been worse, with the fear that he would never see the people he loved again. It was over, at least for now; all he wanted to do was go home and be with his family.

Almost everyone on board the ship had someone awaiting them on the docks and it was difficult for my father to see over all the men's heads as they jockeyed for a position that would allow them to spot their loved ones. He was not a big man, so he was able to squeeze between a few soldiers to stand at the rail to try and catch a glimpse of Peggy. His mind flashed back to Marfa, remembering how wonderful it was when he first saw her and Bobby on the train platform at the air base. He couldn't wait to once again hold her in his arms; it had been over a year since they had said their goodbyes in Casper. As he scanned the excited crowd on the docks, he closed his eyes in prayer, thanking God for bringing him home in one piece. He knew he wanted to make a home with Peggy, have more children, and provide a loving environment in which to raise them. He was determined to make that happen. When he opened his eyes, there she was, waving frantically. His heart leapt into his throat as he waved back like a little school kid. As soon as the ship docked, soldiers began streaming down the gangplank and into the open arms of family and friends. The boat was filled to capacity with returning men and it seemed like an eternity to my father before he was able to disembark. Finally, that embrace he had dreamt of for so long was a dream no more. Tears flowed as they held each other tight. While walking to the car, my dad pressed something small and fluffy into my mom's hand. Bobby's slipper had made its way back home.

They spent the first night in New York City, the beginning of what my mom called a second honeymoon. My dad had been granted a 90-day furlough and they were determined to enjoy every second of it. The next day, they drove back to White Plains, and everyone was waiting for him. He didn't even get a chance to get out of the car before Bobby jumped in his arms; my God how he had grown! He had imagined this moment almost every night at Stalag Luft III; it had given him an inner strength. The most wonderful thing of all was that he no longer had to imagine it; it was happening right now. When he was finally able to put his son down, he gave his mom and dad a huge hug and everyone began talking at once. Peggy's

Atlantic City's Seaside Hotel bill for Bob and
Peggy's second honeymoon, June 1945

parents were also there. He told them how grateful he was for their care of his wife and son during the long and uncertain months of his captivity; he was keenly aware of how much Peggy had leaned on them for support. Eventually, everyone sat down for lunch and my father glowed as he looked around the table at the most important people in his life. It was his first family meal in years and he reveled in it. After lunch, Bobby went back to his grandparents' house and my father and mother headed for Atlantic City for some long overdue time together.

They spent a week there getting reacquainted, at times talking non-stop, and at other times, not talking at all. My dad never spoke about what had happened overseas, so they talked only about happy things, and their plans for the future. They filled their days walking on the beaches and the boardwalk, or they just stayed in their room, as evidenced by the arrival of my brother Bill exactly nine months later. Happy as they were, there was still a cloud of worry—the war that was raging in the Pacific. Once the 90-day leave was over, my father had orders to report back to his squadron. While he found it impossible to talk to my mother about them, memories of the air battle over the Austrian Alps still haunted him. He wondered how he would react if he had to fly bombers again in combat. If only the war would end soon.

Their second honeymoon was wonderful, but they were happy to get back to White Plains. My father discovered something new about Bobby almost every day. His son was barely walking when he had left Casper, and now he couldn't keep up with him. He talked a blue streak, and my mother couldn't help but notice how much happier he was now that his daddy was home. June and July flew by, and before they knew it, my father had only a couple of weeks left before he had to report back to duty. In early August, he began to dread checking his mail, knowing that orders for his redeployment would be arriving shortly.

Like most people, my parents had no idea how long the war in the Pacific would last, and the bombing of Hiroshima and Nagasaki came as a shock. But then, on August 14, 1945, there was cause for great celebration in the Kurtz home as well as in millions of other soldiers' homes throughout the United States—the Japanese had surrendered! The streets of America were filled with deliriously happy people kissing everyone, whether they knew them or not. In what was later to be known as V-J Day, Times Square swelled to capacity with an exuberant crowd like it had never seen. The war had affected nearly every household in one way or another, but now it was over.

On September 22, 1945, my father was relieved of duty at Fort Dix, New Jersey. According to records I found in the green box, his Army Air Force duty had consisted of one year, three months, and ten days of continental service, and 11 months, 20 days of foreign service. He had flown 20 combat missions, accumulating a total of 125 combat hours. He had earned the European African Middle Eastern Theatre Campaign Ribbon with three battle stars. In addition, he was awarded the Purple Heart, the Air Medal, and the American Defense Medal. Including his training at Camp Davis as an artilleryman, he had been a member of the United States Army for four years and two months. Once again a civilian, he looked forward to going on with his life. The exciting news that Peggy was pregnant was a great way to start.

My brother Bill was born on March 14, 1946, at St. Agnes Hospital in White Plains. It had been six months between my father's deactivation and the birth of his second son. In that time, he had found a job in New York City as credit manager for John Powell and Company, an insecticide manufacturer. He was also continuing his college education at New York University, where he took courses at night in order to get enough credits to graduate. On the days he had classes, he would leave home early in the morning and not return until late in the evening. My mother said she never heard him complain once. In reality, being that busy turned out to be a blessing for him; there was no time for him to think about what he had experienced overseas. His family always came first; he loved being picked up at the train station by Peggy and their two boys and talking over the events of the day. The conversation at the dinner table lately had been about the house they were about to close on. My mother was pregnant again, this time with my brother John, and they clearly needed more space. They had found a small three-bedroom house at 9 Ralph Avenue in the Highlands section of White Plains; it would be the first house of their own. A few months after moving in, John was born on August 14, 1947. Everything seemed to be falling in place.

Life at 9 Ralph Avenue was never dull. Raising three young boys filled my mother's days, but she loved being a mom. She looked forward to spending quiet time with my dad after the kids had gone to bed. Even though they were both tired all the time, it was a good type of exhaustion. They had a few friends who they enjoyed having over to play bridge or board games, but they loved just being together, and for the most part, concentrated on raising their family. Two years later, things became even more hectic when their fourth son was welcomed into the world on July 30, 1949.

Bob Kurtz with his four sons at 9 Ralph Avenue, White Plains, New York, 1950

My mother told me that after I was born, she and my father decided not to have any more children. Four boys was certainly more than a handful and they wanted to be able to give each of us the attention we deserved. Finances also played a key part in the decision, with clothing and food expenses being a constant concern, although I never remember being deprived of anything. It was helpful that we were all boys because, unless it was a gift, I don't think I wore anything but hand-me-downs for the first five years of my life. It was different back then, no one cared as long as you had clothing on your back. I don't remember anything of the first two years of my life, but I've been told that my dad was athletic and played ball with my brothers in the backyard. He read us stories and would get up to comfort us if we woke up in the middle of the night. There is a picture of all of us dressed in warm winter coats, standing in front of the house in February of 1952—we were a happy family.

And then, on March 28, all of our lives tragically changed. It was my parents' tenth anniversary and they had gone out for a celebratory dinner. Once home, they came upstairs to kiss each of us goodnight, as they did every night. Back downstairs, my father told my mother that he wasn't feeling well. He thought maybe he had eaten too much because he was experiencing a burning sensation in his chest. They went to bed early. My mother told me that a few hours later she was awakened by my father who had yelled out in pain. Seconds later he was quiet. She tried desperately to waken him but it was too late. He had suffered a massive heart attack and died. He was 33 years old. My mother was 30, and in one moment she had lost the love of her life and become a single mother with four young boys.

FATHERS AND SONS

THERE WAS A LONG GAP BETWEEN THE LAST TIME I CLIMBED the attic stairs of my boyhood home to pore over the contents of the green box, and the point where I picked up the threads to search for my father's story in earnest. It's not that I lost interest in who my father was, but for a while, finding the answers to my questions about him was not a priority. And of course, it was easier to let those questions stay in the background because my brothers and I never felt we could ask about my father. His name rarely came up in conversation, but when it did, my mom's eyes would well up, and none of us ever wanted to make her cry. Although we all missed him terribly, I think losing him was easier on me than anyone in my family, because I was only two years old when he died. Unlike my brothers, who have special memories of him, I do not have any. Days such as Thanksgiving or Christmas were particularly hard on the rest of my family. Listening to a favorite carol or waking up and looking out the window at a blanket of snow on the ground Christmas morning were special events in the Kurtz household, but they also served as stark reminders that we would never be able to share them again with our dad. Not having any memories of spending the holidays with my father was actually a blessing for me. But there was one day a year that was as hard on me as it was on my brothers—Father's Day.

I hated Father's Day while growing up. My mom and my grandparents kept us busy by planning outdoor activities and going out to dinner in the evening. They were kind gestures and well intended, but nothing could make up for the fact that our father was not there to enjoy the festivities with us. I never wanted to go to school the next day; my friends would go into great detail describing how they had taken their dads on fishing trips, hiking adventures, or to a ball game. I remember being incredibly envious, but overall, I never felt sorry for myself. I was raised by a mother who couldn't have loved me more. I was fortunate to have three brothers who looked out for me because I was the youngest. Almost every day of my childhood was happy...every day except the third Sunday in June.

Adolescence in the 1960s in White Plains, New York, was pretty much the same as it was everywhere else at that time. We didn't have a lot of money, but we never lacked for essentials. My brothers and I rode bikes, got part-time jobs, played sports, fell in love with one girl one day and another the next. From as early as I can remember, my mother and grandparents stressed the values of a good education. I loved to read and there was rarely a night I didn't fall asleep with a book in my hand. From about 12 years old, I have fond memories of playing Scrabble with Grandpa Kurtz. He lived five blocks from our house and I would walk there at least once a week for afternoon-long game sessions. He was an editor by profession, and the breadth of his vocabulary was extraordinary. Using a pen, he could polish off the Sunday *New York Times* crossword puzzle in less than an hour. Our Scrabble games were extremely competitive and the thought never entered my grandfather's mind to let me win. I was 17 when I finally beat him and I think he was more excited than I was. He told me how proud my father would have been, which meant the world to me.

My high school years were filled with activities and time flew by. I was fortunate to have excellent teachers who kept me focused on my studies. The competitiveness my grandfather had instilled in me was evident in almost everything I did. I also wanted to please my father, even though he wasn't living. I achieved above-average grades, which made my mother happy, and I'm sure she must have thought about my father with each accomplishment her children made. I looked forward to attending college in the fall of 1967.

I applied to several schools and eventually decided on Gettysburg College, well-known for its beautiful campus and highly respected faculty. In addition, they had offered me the best academic scholarship, and due to our family's financial situation, my decision was an easy one to make. I'm not sure if it was being away from home on my own for the first time, or just lack of effort, but my four years there were a disaster scholastically. It was the first time that I ever really felt that I had let both my parents down. Fortunately, I was able to obtain enough credits to graduate, and thereby became the fourth and last of my brothers to attend and graduate from a four-year college, another accomplishment that made my mother extremely proud.

Almost 50 years later, I discovered that my father had experienced similar problems in college. I knew that he had entered Bowdoin College in Maine in 1936 for his freshman year, but had not returned the next fall. Hoping to find out why, I contacted the archivist there, thinking there might be records that could explain his early exit. I was astounded to find out that there were more than 60 pages of information. Transcripts of his high school and college grades, and letters from my father and my grandfather written to the dean, as well as the dean's return correspondence, gave me an entirely new perspective on my dad. I was surprised to discover that my father had had a tough time with academics at Bowdoin. He had graduated number 45 out of 377 from White Plains High School and his I.Q. score placed him in the top five percent of his freshman class at Bowdoin. But end-of-year records revealed failing grades in several courses. He was obviously an intelligent young man, so I wondered what happened his first year of college that had caused him to have so much trouble with his studies. I tried to put myself in his shoes by remembering what it had been like for me entering my freshman year at Gettysburg, and it all started to make sense.

My grandfather, while a loving parent, was a bit of a taskmaster, and to him, failure of any kind was not an option. I can imagine my dad watching the rear of his father's car disappearing around the bend of the road leading out of Bowdoin. No longer in a busy suburban environment, he took a walk around campus to enjoy the idyllic nature of his surroundings and its magnificent foliage. He relished his newly acquired freedom: being away from home for the first time with so many new things to experience was something he had looked forward to all summer. He decided he would join a fraternity. He had visited the Beta house the previous spring on his campus tour and thought they were a swell bunch of guys. If they pledged him, he would join. The year held great promise for him.

He was concerned with the academic workload, especially his courses in Chemistry and German. He knew his father expected only the best effort and grades from him, but those courses didn't excite him. Only six weeks into his first semester, he wrote his father:

> *Studying incessantly has put me into a terrible state*
> *of mind. I don't have time to get any kind of decent*
> *sleep at all, never getting to bed before twelve at the*

*earliest and then only by sacrificing some of my stud-
ies. There is no time to read, let alone relax. I want to
leave college.*[1]

My grandfather included that letter in correspondence to the dean on November 4, 1936, along with some thoughts of his own: "Bob is inclined to be over serious in a critical situation like this, and to rationalize himself into an unsound position." The remainder of his letter inquired whether tutoring was available, and implored the dean to talk to both my father and his professors. The dean's response must have been an eye-opener for my grandfather:

> *Robert is below passing at this review in his Chem-
> istry, English, German, and Public Speaking. His
> grade in Chemistry is very low, only 27%. In the case
> of English, his low mark of 43% is due very largely,
> says his instructor, to the fact that he has presented
> only two out of eight themes due. In his German, his
> instructor says that his trouble comes through not
> doing his work regularly...I have had two or three
> talks with Bob. Unless he is glad to come back af-
> ter Thanksgiving, and can be counted on utterly to
> change his point of view, and keep out of the dumps,
> it probably would be unwise to have him return. If he
> continues to believe that in his case a college educa-
> tion is superfluous, I see no alternative except letting
> him try a job for a while in the hope that he will see
> the light at the end of another year.*[2]

I'm not quite sure how my father was able to explain this letter to his father, but I'm positive it was not a comfortable conversation. Records show that he returned for the spring semester, and improved his grades somewhat, but chose not to return his sophomore year, even though he had been accepted back. I was amazed at how much his experience mirrored mine. I had also done well academically in high school, but found college more challenging. I was a bit home-sick; I think he may have been as well. I joined a fraternity, as he had, and while I enjoyed the camaraderie, late nights at the Sigma Alpha Epsilon house led to bad study habits and poor attendance in class. I, too, wrote a letter home saying how unhappy I was and that

I wanted to transfer or come home. Knowing that my father had also had trouble with his courses bonded me to him even further. Finding out that he was not perfect made me love him even more.

After graduation, I dabbled at a variety of jobs, mostly in the food service business as a bartender, waiter, and maître d'. I met my future wife, Audrey, in the restaurant where I worked and we were married a couple of years later. Our son Michael was born on May 13, 1981, followed by a second son, Brian, on July 12, 1983. We were blessed with two healthy children to bring up. Becoming a father put a new perspective on life for me; Father's Day was now a day to celebrate, not ignore.

I began to think more and more about my dad as my sons grew older. There were times I felt sad that he could not see the father I had become. My mother told me that my dad had been a wonderful parent and as I watched my boys grow up, I was obsessed with providing them the same love I know that he would have given me, had he lived. They are now grown men, successful in life, and have given me more joy than I could ever have hoped for.

As I began to explore his life, I became intrigued with the wartime experiences of Robert R. Kurtz and decided to attempt to duplicate them as much as was realistically possible. In 2001, I purchased a book entitled *The 465th "Remembered"*, by Gene Moxley. Inside were more than 20 pages describing the events of August 3, 1944, including debriefings of each of the crewmen on *Sugar Baby* in which they described the events of the bombing mission that had ended in disaster. My father's account was particularly detailed and it made me feel as if I actually had been inside the ill-fated bomber. Obviously, there was no way to duplicate his combat experiences as a co-pilot, so I set out to do the next best thing. I had heard of a group known as the Collings Foundation that offered flights on the only B-24 Liberator in the world that was still in working order. They fly to different airports around the country and I was surprised to find out they were soon to be in my area, so I immediately made reservations. On the day of the air show, I stood mesmerized as the vintage Liberator set down on the tarmac, wondering how many hundreds of times my dad had practiced that landing during training.

Climbing up into the plane was surreal, and the first thing that struck me was the cramped quarters. I wondered what it must have been like for my father and the crewmen of *Sugar Baby* as they desperately tried to escape the burning inferno inside their Liberator. The noise produced at takeoff was deafening and the bomber vibrated intensely as it strained to climb into the sky. Once airborne, we were able to move about the plane, and I immediately headed for the nose. We were not allowed in the cockpit, but I did crawl into the bombardier's position. I marveled at the bravery it must have taken for George Britton to remain calm as he sighted in on targets during bombing missions. He once told me that deadly puffs of flak bursts exploding in the skies around him were sometimes so thick that "it looked like you could walk on them."

We had flown out of Westchester County Airport in White Plains on a dreary, rainy day in late July 2001. Our flight path took us down the Hudson River over the George Washington Bridge, past the Empire State Building, and around the Statue of Liberty. As we swung back north, I sat in the Plexiglas enclosure of the bombardier's position and stared directly at the twin towers of the World Trade Center rising majestically out of lower Manhattan, having no idea that terrorist attacks of fewer than two months later would never allow me that opportunity again. As we headed back northward over the Hudson, I decided to explore the tail end of the bomber. I crossed the catwalk between the bomb bays, past the two side gunner positions in the main fuselage, and headed for the tail gunner's position. I tried to imagine what it had been like to be in such a tight space during combat, knowing that your position was the most vulnerable to attack from enemy fighters. And then I remembered. The debriefings I had read in Moxley's book differed in many ways but agreed on one detail. All recalled that Charlie Sellars, a replacement tail gunner on *Sugar Baby* that day, was grievously injured during the air battle and was unable to exit the plane before it crashed into the Austrian Alps. Standing there, looking at the same spot where on a different bomber a brave young man had lost his life was a very sobering experience.

The following month, I had another opportunity to step into my father's shoes in Austria, at the commemoration of the air battle over Ehrwald. We hiked up the Brendlkar, site of *Sugar Baby's* crash. Gerd Leitner showed me where my dad had been captured by German soldiers and the tiny inn where the American airmen had been held at gunpoint. Had my father followed the same path down that we had taken, or had he clung to the underbrush to avoid detection? That evening, I heard Hilde Richter's riveting account of my dad's capture, and I wondered whether I would have been able to keep my cool as he had.

Returning home, I continued my quest to simulate my father's wartime experiences. Eight years later, in the summer of 2009, I visited my mom at Brooksby Village, an assisted living facility in Peabody, Massachusetts, where she lived for many years. She was 88 years old and although she was healthy and of sound mind, I knew that it was important for me to ask questions about my dad sooner rather than later. After we talked, my mom got up and said she had something for me. A couple of minutes later, she returned with a wallet in her hand. "I knew I had this somewhere," she said. "I just wasn't sure where. It was your father's; I put it away the night your dad died and haven't looked at it since." I was stunned. We didn't go through it together; even though it had been 57 years since my dad had died, I knew looking at the contents would only sadden her, so I waited until I got home. The first card I pulled from his wallet read:

```
This is to certify that Lt. Robert R. Kurtz
is a member of the Caterpillar Club whose
life was spared the 3 day of August 1944
because of an emergency parachute jump
from an aircraft. Membership certificate
has been issued to the end that this
safety medium in the art of flying may be
furthered. Date of issue: 1-27-47.
```

I remembered one of the contents in the green box had been a tiny metal pin in the curved shape of a caterpillar. I knew it wasn't a military decoration and had no idea why it was in the box—now the mystery was solved. I realized that the first card I pulled out wasn't a coincidence; it felt like a sign, and I knew what I needed to do. My father had done it on August 3, 1944, albeit unwillingly, and on August 3, 2009, it would be my turn—to jump out of a plane.

My sixtieth birthday was at the end of July and I had already made plans to celebrate with my two sons at Mike's house in Phoenix, Arizona. We were going to play a lot of golf and just enjoy being together. When I told them that I was going to add a sky dive to the agenda, they were a little surprised, but understood how important it was to me. Knowing they had both already done it, I asked them if they wanted to join me, hoping that at least one of them would come along to lend a little moral support. We all knew I was terrified of heights. Understandably, Mike declined because my granddaughter, Ashley, had just been born. Brian, on the other hand, was up for another jump.

When the day arrived, although excited, I had to own up to a serious case of frayed nerves. I brought an array of things for good luck, including the famous baby slipper, the caterpillar pin, my dad's dog tags, and the pilot's wings he had earned at Marfa. We were videotaping, so after dedicating the sky dive to my father and my brother, John, who had recently passed away, the door opened at 12,500 feet. It was a tandem jump and I felt my instructor's knee jam into my back, reminding me that it was now or never. For a split second, I felt myself transported back in time to 1944 and *I am co-pilot, 2nd Lt. Robert R. Kurtz, preparing to bail out of a burning bomber, with only the will to survive propelling me out of the plane. Injured and scared out of my wits, I try to put out the flames on*

Jim Kurtz and sky diving tandem instructor, Mesa, Arizona, Summer 2009

*my bomber jacket before I jump. I have never parachuted out of an
aircraft. If that isn't enough, on the ground, German soldiers are
everywhere waiting for me to drift down, or even worse, to shoot
me as I dangle in the sky above.* After thinking about what my father
had endured, it was easy for me to jump. It was exhilarating! The
connection I felt to my father as I plummeted earthward is almost
impossible to explain. Upon safely setting down, the first thing I did
was reach into my pocket and squeeze the baby slipper, as my dad

must have done many years before—it
was *my* lucky charm this time.

I was surprised at how much more I
learned about my father from the contents of his wallet. His business card revealed that, at the time of his death, he
was credit manager for John Powell &
Co., Inc., an insecticide manufacturer located on Park Avenue in New York City.
In addition, there were the usual items
such as his driver's license, Social Security card, railway pass, and even a small
grocery list. One of the last things I came
across was a laminated identification card
dated May 28, 1945. On the front was a
photograph of my father, very thin, deeply
tanned, unshaven, and not smiling. It
had been taken by the War Department
on the day he ar-
rived in the States
from Le Havre.
When I compared
it to pictures of my
dad taken before
his deployment, it
was painful to see
what ten months of
combat and impris-
onment had done to

Images from 1942 (above) and 1945 (below) offer poignant proof of how
combat, internment in POW camps, and The Long March affected my father

him. My mother told me numerous times that my father never spoke to her or anyone about what had happened overseas. It was obvious that he wanted, or more importantly, needed, to put the horror of war behind him. And yet he carried his military discharge photo in his wallet when his driver's license would have been more than sufficient as identification. I think he found himself mired in the conundrum of trying to forget, but unable to, or perhaps not really wanting to.

I remember asking my mother a few years ago, after watching a documentary on PTSD (Post-Traumatic Stress Disorder), if she thought my father had displayed any of its tendencies upon returning home from overseas. Post-WWII psychologists used terms such as "shell shock" and "battle fatigue" but their symptoms were basically the same. Her answer surprised me. She said he was determined to pick up his life where it had left off before his deployment. Ecstatic to be reunited with his wife and son, the joys of being home must have overshadowed his memories of war. Outwardly, he maintained a great disposition and, according to my mom, never exhibited the mood swings that can define PTSD. Inwardly, it's anyone's guess as to how it affected his mental health. Clearly, the starvation and illness that were a part of POW life, and more significantly, the Long March, had taken a huge physical toll. The autopsy performed after his death revealed a severely weakened heart. The medical examiner who performed the procedure determined his fatal heart attack was a direct result of the abuse his body had taken during his nine months of imprisonment. It was a critically important diagnosis because it meant that my mother would receive monthly checks from the Veterans Administration until all of her children had reached adulthood.

The Veterans Administration checks helped my mother pay some of the bills, but they weren't nearly enough to cover the costs of raising four children and owning a home. An act of kindness by my father in 1945, one that my mother was unaware of until after his death, would allow us to remain at 9 Ralph Avenue. A friend of his from White Plains, who had also served overseas, was in the insurance field. Although he really couldn't afford it, my father took out a mortgage insurance policy as a favor and filed it away. The day after my dad died, my mother was going through his papers, and came across the policy. She called my father's buddy and was told that her mortgage would be paid off in full. Fittingly, even though he was gone, my dad was still helping my mom.

But there were other bills to be paid, and food and clothing to buy, and the first few years were difficult for my mother. Both sets of my grandparents lived in White Plains and helped her financially when they were able to, but it was clear that once I entered kindergarten, she would have to find employment. She got a secretarial job in the school system, so that her working hours would coincide with the hours we were in school. From that point on, she worked every year until her retirement in 1981. To supplement that income, she sold tickets at high school football games and proctored college entrance exams on weekends. She became my role model and my inspiration. What I remember most about her was that she never complained about having to work, she just did it. She was always exhausted, and yet, somehow found time to love and care for her children, whom she had to be both mother and father to. Thankfully, she passed her work ethic on to her children, which helped me immensely in my career.

When I told my mom I was going to write a book that would pri-marily be about my father, she began to open up a little more about him. She was proud of what I was doing and started sharing stories with me about my dad. In May of 2010, I gave a speech at Brooksby Village. It was about my search for the fa-ther I had never known. My mom was 89 years old at the time and could still get around fairly well for her

Peggy Kurtz, age 75

age, and yet she chose to watch my speech from her apartment on closed circuit television rather than go to the auditorium to see me in person. And I totally understood. It had been 58 years since she had lost her husband, and although understanding and supportive of my journey to find my dad, she still felt his loss deeply. Attending my speech would have been too hard for her; her living room was the perfect place for her to proudly watch her son, cry a few tears, and not have to share her emotions with anyone else. After the speech, I visited her and we shared a hug I will never forget. She passed away on March 27, 2012, at the age of 90. She was my rock, my pillar of strength, and there isn't a day that goes by that I don't think of her.

Although it feels like I have reached the end of my journey, the reality is that if we are lucky, we are always learning about the people we love. When I originally set out to discover who my father was, I had very little information to work with. Every day I regret not having talked to my mother more about my dad, especially once I reached adulthood. Fortunately, she did write an autobiography, "Letter to My Grandchildren," which was a critical source of information for parts of this book.

Of my father, I have no memories at all. It is still strange to see pictures of him holding me in his arms, and I've always wished I could have remembered those moments. I was two years old when he died; I doubt many adults can recall much of anything at that age. What I do remember is a particular scent that I must have inhaled when he was still living. It was from the talcum powder he used after shaving. It wasn't until years later that I was able to make the connection. I was 16 years old and sitting in a barber shop, treating myself to a shave, and as my barber patted talc on my neck, I sensed the association between the powder's scent and my father. I took notice of the color, shape, and brand name of its container and when I got home, asked my mom if my dad had ever used talcum powder after shaving. She said, "Yes. Every day," and before she had the chance to tell me what the brand name was, I already knew it would be the same as the one that had been applied to my face that morning.

The small memories pile up. I know the words from the iconic songs of the 1940s, even some of the obscure ones. Songs like "Chattanooga Choo Choo" are an essential part of the sound track of my life. My parents shared a love for music and dancing, and the radio or phonograph was playing all the time in our home. After my father died, I can recall my mother crying every time the song "Apple Blossom Time" would come on. And there were occasional stories that came out. My mom would point out planes as they flew over our house with vapor trails streaking out behind them and explain how it brought back fond memories of the months she and my dad had lived in Casper, Wyoming, during his flight training. There, she would hear the roar of the bombers' engines and run outside to look up in the sky, knowing that her husband was flying one of those airplanes. I still watch for those vapor trails.

For many years, songs, sights, and smells were all I had to connect myself to my father, and while they were better than nothing at all, what was clearly missing was a definition of his character. The discovery of the green box changed that. Reading letters and telegrams he sent home during his captivity brought him alive to me. His "Twenty-Four Hours of Flight" gave me the first glimpse into his combat experiences, as well as an admiration for his writing skills. Then years later, my trips to Austria opened the floodgates. Each interview with not only his friends but also his enemies, offered me more pieces of the puzzle that made up Robert Kurtz. And when I learned about his struggles in college, so like my own, I saw, too, how perhaps even for me, "the apple did not fall far from the tree."

There are mysteries still, things I would like to know, but in what parent-child relationship is that not true? There was a time when I thought I would never know my father as more than a picture in a frame, dating from a time I could not remember. Yet because I opened a green box when I was a curious child, and picked it up again decades later, and because I was aided by amazing people who were a part of his story, I went from knowing nothing about my dad to knowing him as if he were still alive. I have come to learn a little bit about him as a husband and a loving father. He saved a man's life, yet never spoke of it—an unassuming hero if there ever was one. The information I have uncovered over the past few years about my father has made him my hero. I have established a relationship with him that, while it doesn't make up for missing him in my childhood, or fulfill my desire to sit and talk with him for hours and hours, is something authentic. I went to search for my father and in so doing, found myself. As he said, "it's hard to know where it begins and where it ends." He was talking about combat missions; it's also true about life.

Jim with his sons, pictured left to right, Brian and Michael

ACKNOWLEDGMENTS

F IRST, I WOULD LIKE TO THANK TWO HIGHLY ACCOMPLISHED and well-respected men in the literary field who urged me to put down on paper the story of my quest to find out more about my father. They are author and newsman, the late Tim Russert, and author and *Boston Globe* columnist, Kevin Cullen.

I am proud to be one of the contributing authors in Russert's book, *Wisdom of Our Fathers*. I met Tim at a book signing event at the Newton Free Library outside of Boston in June 2006. He told me that he felt my story was book-worthy. I never forgot that. In 2010, I contacted Kevin Cullen, telling him a story about my trip to Austria which had uncovered additional information about my father. He liked the story enough to write a column entitled, "Decades later, war's chapter completed," which appeared in the September 19, 2010 edition of the Sunday *Boston Globe*. Coincidentally, I was at one of his book signings when he encouraged me to pursue my aspirations of writing a book about my father. It was an honor and a privilege to have met both of them.

I can honestly say this book would never have become a reality without my wife, Julie's, belief in my project. Throughout the over two years' time I worked on this book, she was my constant companion as an understanding wife, editor, consultant, researcher, and most importantly, best friend. The hundreds of hours she spent at her computer helping me with the book were an unexpected plus. She is also a fine artist, noteworthy because the cover and design of *The Green Box* are a product of her creative vision.

As far as the actual contents of the book, its flow and its integrity, I owe an enormous debt of gratitude to my writing coach and mentor, Victoria Hughes. We met at a local writers' club in Ipswich, Massachusetts, and quickly became friends. I am awed by her knowledge of the English language; I can only describe her vocabulary as being other-worldly. Our discussions on when to use hyphens, commas, and semi-colons were lengthy and painful, but always enlightening and in good fun. Over the past two years, her dedication and belief in my book have helped immensely in keeping me focused on the project. She has become more than a good friend; in many ways, she has become a part of our family.

All along the way, it has been a family affair. After-dinner discussions with my wife's son, Brian Gressler, were most helpful. He offered organizational tips during the early stages of this daunting project, while thoughtfully providing insight and guidance as to how the story should be told.

His sister, Jeanne Koles, freely gave her time with readings and comments on early drafts. With her expertise as an art book director and designer, she brought the book cover and contents to life in a beautiful and professional package.

My brother Bill's contribution should not be forgotten. Starting in the late 1990s, he began an intensive Internet search into our father's military past. He purchased pertinent war records and eventually located and was able to speak with some of the original members of the crew that had trained and fought with our dad during WWII. His enthusiasm was contagious and his willingness to share information was the jumpstart I needed.

Acting on advice from Victoria Hughes, I hired Karen McCarthy for the final edit. Vicki told me she was meticulous in her editing; that was an understatement. She added some sorely-needed punctuation corrections, while, thankfully, extracting more than just a few of my over-worked adverbs. Above all, she never tried to change my "voice," and for that, I will be forever thankful to her.

I am grateful to Allyson Skinner for finding the time to read my manuscript and offer suggestions while balancing the duties of wife, mother, and full-time employment. I have known Ally a long time; she is a good friend and an even better editor.

Thanks to author Marilyn Walton for answering my endless questions on Stalag Luft III and "The Long March." Her knowledge of those two subjects is well-documented and recognized by numerous WWII military historians; her suggestions and corrections were extremely helpful.

Sadly, three crew members that flew combat missions with my father overseas have passed away since I began writing *The Green Box*. I traveled to the homes of George Britton, Joe Spontak, and Tony Jezowski to learn more about my father's wartime experiences with them. Their hospitality quickly made me feel at home. Their recollections of times spent with my father, both in the States and overseas, were invaluable. Those memories made my dad come to life, allowing me to obtain a much clearer picture of what type of man he was. Thank you, and rest in peace, gentlemen.

The chapter, "Bringing Charlie Home," could not have been written without the combined effort and help of Carole Williams, Ken Sellars, Janet Sellars, and Debbie Cooke. Carole tracked down the names of Charles Sellars' living siblings, which eventually led me to his brother Ken. Ken's and Janet's willingness to share stories and memories of Charlie, as well as Debbie's contribution of correspondence and photographs, were key factors in helping me come to know him as an individual and not just the tail gunner on my father's B-24.

I owe a debt of gratitude to Pat Logan, Jr. and John Goss, who provided me with a more precise picture of the hardships and perils of heavy bomber flight training at Casper Army Air Base from 1943–1944.

I cannot emphasize enough what a huge role Gerd Leitner played in the formation of this book. Without his invitation to the commemoration in Ehrwald, Austria, in 2001, I doubt if *The Green Box* would ever have become a reality.

I would sincerely like to thank Debbie Beson for sharing stories of her father with me, and more importantly, for urging me to make the trip to Ehrwald in 2001.

A heartfelt thanks goes out to Steve Wiley, Brigadier General Jim Anderson, and Angela Sontheimer, all elite staff members at the Lincoln Leadership Institute in Gettysburg, Pennsylvania. Their support of my book-writing project provided a sorely needed shot in the arm more than once in the past two years.

Finally, I would like to acknowledge and sincerely thank all the men and women that have served or are presently serving in the Armed Forces, many of whom made the supreme sacrifice to ensure the freedom and democracy that we embrace in this country today.

ENDNOTES

All correspondence, unless otherwise noted, is from the collection belonging to Margaret Kurtz, and after her death, her heirs. Much of the anecdotal wartime information derives from my numerous conversations with George Britton and Joe Spontak.

Chapter 2: And So It All Began

1. www.skylighters.org/places/cd5.html
2. North Carolina Highway Historical Marker Program www.ncmarkers.com/Markers.aspx?MarkerId=C-65
3. Kurtz Family Archive
4. My dad's account was originally published in the *Inglewood Daily News*, a California local paper. It was then picked up by an editor at *The Atlantic Monthly*. I have a reprint of *The Atlantic Monthly* version, which appeared in an ongoing column called "Atlantic Bookshelf."
5. Kurtz Family Archive
6. www.nationalmuseum.af.mil/factsheets/factsheet.asp?id=499
7. www.nationalmuseum.af.mil/factsheets/factsheet.asp?id=481
8. Texas State Historical Association www.tshaonline.org/handbook/onlline/articles/qcm01
9. www.en.wikipedia.org/wiki/Marfa_Army_Air_Field
10. www.classicwarbirds.net/1942-cessna-t-50-bamboo-bomber
11. Kurtz Family Archive. This was taken from the White Plains local paper of the time, *The Reporter Dispatch*. I only have the cutout clipping itself, but the date of publication would be sometime in May 1943. It was a fairly common practice for local newspapers to report the comings and goings of local servicemen.
12. Kurtz Family Archive
13. http://trib.com/news/local/casper-wwii-fire-truck-brings-history-home/article_016f26d3-e786-50d4-802b-d2b92ab11e45.html
14. www.en.wikipedia.org/wiki/Casper-Natrona_County_International_Airport
15. http://trib.com/news/local/casper-wwii-fire-truck-brings-history-home/article_016f26d3-e786-50d4-802b-d2b92ab11e45.html
16. ibid
17. The source for this data is from a phone conversation with John Goss, the director of the Wyoming Veterans Memorial Museum.
18. The debriefing statements are from US Army Air Force documents entitled, "Report of Aircraft Accident 14 May 1944," copies of which are held at The Wyoming Veterans Museum and provided to me by the director, John Goss.
19. The details of this incident are still emerging. The original documents were classified and at this point we only have the story from Pat Logan, Sr., who told the story to his son.
20. http://www.nebraskastudies.org/0800/frameset_reset.html?http://www.nebraskastudies.org/0800/stories/0801_0108.html
21. http://www.usaaf.net/digest/t213.htm

Chapter 3: Ehrwald

1. This is from the piece that Hilde Richter handed out at the commemoration in 2001.

Chapter 4: Deadly Skies
1. There are numerous sites with detailed WWII bomber flight statistics and casualties, and while they don't all agree exactly, they do fall into the same range. http://www.defense.gov/news/newsarticle.aspx?id=122154
2. http://www.defense.gov/news/newsarticle.aspx?id=122154
3. http://en.wikipedia.org/wiki/Bombing_of_Friedrichshafen_in_World_War_II
4. http://www.merriam-webster.com/dictionary/flak
5. http://www.constable.ca/caah/flak.htm
6. ibid
7. http://www.britannica.com/EBchecked/topic/72612/bombsight
8. Frederick A. Johnsen, WARBIRDTECH Series, Volume 1, Consolidated B-24 Liberator (Specialty Press 1996), p.6
9. Gene F. Moxley, *The 465th "Remembered" Book II*, p.189. This book is a compilation of declassified military documents and debriefings.
10. ibid, p.S
11. ibid, p.O
12. ibid, p.335

Chapter 5: Captivity
1. http://www.486th.org/Photos/Stammlager/KU3738/DulagLuft.htm
2. http://en.wikipedia.org/wiki/Dulag_Luft
3. http://www.merkki.com/new_page_2.htm
4. ibid
5. ibid
6. http://www.486th.org/Photos/Stammlager/KU3738/DulagLuft.htm
7. ibid
8. http://usmilitary.about.com/library/milinfo/genevacon/blart-17.htm
9. http://www.486th.org/Photos/Stammlager/KU3738/DulagLuft.htm
10. Marilyn Jeffers Walton, *Rhapsody in Junk*, p.123
11. ibid
12. http://en.wikipedia.org/wiki/Stalag_Luft_III
13. ibid
14. http://www.usafa.edu/df/dflib/SL3/SL3.cfm?catname=Dean%20of%20Faculty
15. Robert Kurtz transcription of a quote from Churchill's biography, *Winston Churchill, My Early Life: 1874-1904*, p.259. An online edition is available: https://archive.org/details/rovingcommissino001321mbp
16. http://en.wikipedia.org/wiki/Stalag_Luft_III
17. ibid
18. ibid
19. Donald L. Miller, *Masters of the Air: America's Bomber Boys Who Fought the Air War Against Nazi Germany*, p.390
20. http://www.merkki.com/documents.htm
21. http://en.wikipedia.org/wiki/Hermann_G%C3%B6ring
22. http://en.wikipedia.org/wiki/Stalag_Luft_III
23. http://www.redcross.org.uk/About-us/Who-we-are/Museum-and-archives/Historical-factsheets/Food-parcels
24. http://en.wikipedia.org/wiki/Stalag_Luft_III
25. http://www.merkki.com/the_guards.htm
26. The original of this letter belongs to Debbie Beson.
27. http://www.stalagluft4.org/luft%204%20reports.html

28. http://www.trasksdad.com/PopsProgress/march_1.htm

Chapter 6: The March Home
1. Bob Neary, *Stalag Luft III: A Collection of German Prison Camp Sketches with Descriptive Text Based on Personal Experiences*, p.1. This is a self-published text from 1946.
2. http://www.trasksdad.com/PopsProgress/march_1.htm
3. ibid
4. http://www.b24.net/pow/stalag3.htm
5. Kenneth Simmons, *Kriegie: Prisoner of War*, Kindle edition, location 3011 of 4425
6. ibid, location 3026 of 4425
7. Andrew Turner, "Death March of the Kriegies," *44th Bomber Group Veterans Association*, Issue 1, Summer 2005. www.8thairforce.com/44thbg/8balltails/Vol%207%20Issue%201%20Summer%202005.pdf
8. http://en.wikipedia.org/wiki/Forty-and-eights
9. Kenneth Simmons, *Kriegie: Prisoner of War*, Kindle edition, location 3648
10. http://www.b24.net/pow/stalag13.htm
11. Bob Neary, *Stalag Luft III: A Collection of German Prison Camp Sketches with Descriptive Text Based on Personal Experiences*. I have a reprint of the original, but not all the pages are numbered.
12. ibid
13. http://en.wikipedia.org/wiki/The_March_%281945%29
14. Bob Neary, *Stalag Luft III: A Collection of German Prison Camp Sketches with Descriptive Text Based on Personal Experiences*, p.42
15. http://www.8thairforce.com/44thbg/8balltails/Vol.%207%20Issue%201%20Summer%202005.pdf
16. John Nichol and Tony Rennell, *The Last Escape*, p.276
17. www.burrcook.com/wwii/rabc11.html
18. http://www.moosburg.org/info/stalag/murphyeng.html
19. http://www.skylighters.org/special/cigcamps/
20. ibid
21. ibid
22. http://www.med-dept.com/articles/r-a-m-p/
23. http://forum.armyairforces.com/Camp-Lucky-Strike-m74412.aspx
24. ibid
25. ibid
26. http://military.wikia.com/wiki/Advanced_Service_Rating_Score

Chapter 8: Bringing Charlie Home
Charles Sellars' niece, Debbie Cooke, provided me with copies of all correspondence concerning her uncle. Those quoted in this chapter come from her collection.
1. http://www.orangeblossom.ca/about_orange.asp

Chapter 10: Fathers and Sons
1. Copies of the correspondence between my grandfather and the Dean of Bowdoin College were provided by the George J. Mitchell Department of Special Collections + Archives at the Bowdoin College Library. 3000 College Station, Brunswick, Maine 04011 | 207.725.3385
2. ibid

BIBLIOGRAPHY

Print:

Ambrose, Stephen E. *The Wild Blue*. New York: Simon and Schuster, 2001.

Bowman, Martin W. *B-24 Combat Missions*. London: Metro Books, 2009.

Frater, Stephen. *Hell Above Earth*. New York: St. Martin's Press, 2012.

Johnsen, Frederick A. *Consolidated B-24 Liberator*. Minnesota: Specialty Press, 1996.

Moxley, Gene F. *Missing in Action*. 1st Books, 2002.

Moxley Gene F., comp. *The 465ᵗʰ "Remembered" Book II*. Self-Published.

Neary, Bob. *Stalag Luft III: A Collection of German Prison Camp Sketches with Descriptive Text Based on Personal Experiences*. North Wales, PA: Thomason Press, Inc., 1946.

Nichol, John and Tony Rennell. *The Last Escape*. New York: Viking, 2002.

Rutkowski, William F. *We Regret to Inform You....* Salt Lake City, UT: Aardvark Global Publishing LLC, 2001 (2006).

Simmons, Kenneth. *Kriegie: Prisoner of War*. Edited by Steve Chadde. Uncommon Valor Press, 2014. Kindle edition.

Storrow, Benjamin. "Casper WWII fire truck brings history home." *Casper Star Tribune Communications*. Casper, Wyoming. May 26, 2013.

Walton, Marilyn Jeffers. *Rhapsody In Junk: A Daughter's Return to Germany to Finish Her Father's Story*. Bloomington, IN: Author House, 2007.

Walton, Marilyn Jeffers and Michael C. Eberhardt. *From Interrogation to Liberation: A Photographic Journey: Stalag Luft III-The Road to Freedom*. Bloomington, IN: Author House, 2014.

Online:

44th Bomb Group Veterans Association, Volume 7. Accessed January 2014. http://www.8thairforce.com.

"Advanced Service Rating Score." Accessed August 2014. http://military.wikia.com/wiki/Advanced_Service_Rating_Score.

"Berga: Soldiers of Another War." Accessed May 2013. http://www.pbs.org.

"Bombing of Friedrichshafen in World War II." http://www.wikipedia.org.

"Camp Lucky Strike." Accessed September 2013. http://forum.armyairforces.com/Camp-Lucky-Strike-m77412.aspx.

"Casper–Natrona County International Airport." http://www.wikipedia.org.

"Dulag Luft." http://www.wikipedia.org.

"Food Parcels in the Second World War." Accessed May 2013. http://www.redcross.org.uk/About-us/Who-we-are/Museum-and-archives/ Historical-factsheets/Food-parcels.

"Forty-and-eights." http://www.wikipedia.org.

"German Anti-aircraft Flak." Canadian Air Aces and Heroes. http://www.constable.ca.

"Hermann Göring." http://www.wikipedia.org.

Introducing Camp Davis: History. Accessed June 2014. http://www.skylighters.org/places/cd5.html.

Lyle, Amaani, "World War II Internment Camp Survivors Honored 70 Years Later." *DoD Newsletter. U.S. Department of Defense.* April 30, 2014. http://www.defense.gov/newsarticle.aspx?id=122154.

"Marfa Army Air Field." http://www.wikipedia.org.

Murphy, Frank D. "The Liberation of Moosburg." Moosburg Online. Accessed March 2014. http://www.moosburg.org/info/stalag/murphyeng.html.

National Museum of the US Air Force. Fact Sheets. http://www.nationalmuseum. af.mil/factsheets/factsheet.asp?id=499.

"Nebraska Army Airfields." http://www.nebraskastudies.org/0800/frameset_ reset.html?http://www.nebraskastudies.org/0800/stories/0801_0108.html.

North Carolina Department of Cultural Resources. http://www.ncmarkers.com/Home.aspx.

Photorecon: Online Magazine for Aviation Enthusiasts. http://classicwarbirds. net/1942-cessna-t-50-bamboo-bomber.

"RAMP." WW2 US Medical Research Center. Accessed July 2014. http://www.med-dept.com/articles/r-a-m-p/.

"Stalag Luft 3." Accessed January 2014. http://www.b24.net/pow/stalag3.htm.

"Stalag Luft III." http://www.wikipedia.org.

Stalag Luft VI and IV. http://www.stalagluft4.org.

"The Guards." Stalag Luft 1 Online. http://www.merkki.com/new_page_2.htm.

"The Interrogators." Stalag Luft 1 Online. www.merkki.com/new_page_2.htm.

"The March (1945)." http://www.wikipedia.org.

The United States Air Force Academy. "The Story of Stalag Luft III." Accessed October 23, 2014. http://www.usafa.edu/df/dflib/SL3/ SL3cfm?catname=Dean%20of%Faculty.

Wilson, D.E.L. "The March from Luft III." Accessed June 2001. http://www.trasksdad.com/PopsProgress/march_1.htm.